SCHOLASTIC

YOU CAN

Teach Phonics

Wendy Jolliffe

FOR AGES
3-7

Systematic phonics teaching
eds to be carefully planned…
secure children's progress. "

(Dfes)

Acknowledgements

Author
Wendy Jolliffe

Illustrations
Q2A Media

Development Editor
Simret Brar

Series Designer
Catherine Perera

Editor
Vicky Butt

Designer
Q2A Media

Assistant Editor
Alex Albrighton

Cover Designer
Catherine Perera

Text © 2007 Wendy Jolliffe
© 2007 Scholastic Ltd

Designed using Adobe InDesign

Published by Scholastic Ltd
Villiers House
Clarendon Avenue
Leamington Spa
Warwickshire CV32 5PR

www.scholastic.co.uk

Printed by Bell and Bain Ltd.
2 3 4 5 6 7 8 9   8 9 0 1 2 3 4 5 6

The publishers gratefully acknowledge permission to reproduce the following copyright material:

Celia Warren for the use of 'Red Rag Rabbit' by Celia Warren © 2007, Celia Warren (2007, previoulsy unpublished).
Her Majesty's Stationery Office for the use of extracts from http://www.standards.dfes.gov.uk/primary/ © Crown copyright, reproduced under the terms of the Click-Use Licence.

Every effort has been made to trace copyright holders for the works reproduced in this book, and the publishers apologise for any inadvertent omissions.

British Library Cataloguing-in-Publication Data
A catalogue record for this book is available from the British Library.
ISBN 978-0439-94554-7

Contents

Contents

Introduction

This book provides clear guidance on teaching phonics in accordance with the latest recommendations from the *Primary National Strategy* and the *Rose Review* of the teaching of reading. Research has shown that daily systematic phonics teaching has a significant impact on children's reading ability. However, to be effective, the teacher should first assess that children have developed the ability to hear and discriminate individual sounds. This can be supported through the use of rhyme, rhythm and alliteration – and, in addition, children need to learn the alphabet sequence and letter names. Teaching alphabet songs (for example, to the tune of 'Twinkle Twinkle Little Star') can also be very beneficial. Children need to know that letters have names as well as representing sounds, so the letter 'B' has a name and makes the sound /b/. Alphabetic awareness is an important factor in becoming a proficient reader and therefore should be included within the early stages of phonics teaching.

As soon as children have acquired the ability to discriminate sounds, phonics should be taught quickly. The teaching should be lively and multi-sensory, and provide regular practice of applying the phonemes learned to reading and spelling. Tracking children's progress is vital to ensure that those needing reinforcement are supported when necessary. *You Can... Teach Phonics* supports all of these and covers the following key aspects:

- developing phonological awareness
- learning all consonant, short and long vowel phonemes and their common spellings
- linking phonics to work on speaking and listening, reading and writing.

You Can... Teach Phonics is linked to *Phonics: A Complete Synthetic Programme* by Wendy Jolliffe (Scholastic Ltd), but while it complements this detailed programme, it also provides stand-alone guidance that will support both experienced and less-experienced teachers in ensuring effective teaching of phonics. As recommended by the *Rose Review*, the key aspects of synthetic phonics are that all phonemes are taught systematically alongside learning to blend the letters for reading and to segment words into the corresponding phonemes, which is needed for spelling.

How to use this book

You Can... Teach Phonics provides guidance and activities for all aspects of effective phonics teaching. This will be useful for teachers, teaching assistants and for parents and carers. The activities within each chapter can be selected, as appropriate, to reinforce other teaching and will be particularly useful to support those with limited experience of teaching phonics. Each page beings with an italicised introduction that provides background information and places the activities in the context of an effective phonics programme.

- The 'Thinking points' raise issues of resources and provide general advice and pointers or questions to support the teaching of phonics.
- The 'Tips, ideas and activities' section provides a range of activities and ideas for use with children.
- Finally, the photcopiable pages at the back of the book provide resources to support teaching as well as assessing children's progress.

This book is not a complete phonics programme and is intended to support work alongside such a programme. Commencing with support on ensuring phonological awareness – the essential pre-requisite of being able to hear and discriminate sounds – *You Can... Teach Phonics* provides guidance on teaching all phonemes systematically using a synthetic approach. Guidance is also provided on the correct pronunciation of sounds. The importance of ensuring that children develop good oral skills is emphasised throughout and much of this is supported by encouraging partner work.

A further key aspect of this book is to ensure tracking of children's progress by providing a range of diagnostic assessment tools.

Key terms

The following terms are used:
- **Phoneme:** a phoneme is the smallest single identifiable sound, eg the letters 'ch' representing one sound /ch/
- **Grapheme:** a grapheme is a letter, or a series of letters that represents a phoneme (the spelling)
- **Graph:** one letter representing a phoneme (h/a/t contains three graphs)
- **Digraph:** two letters representing a phoneme (l/i/ck) contains two graphs and one digraph)
- **Split digraph:** two letters making one phoneme, split by a consonant, eg '/m/a/k/e'
- **Trigraph:** three letters representing a phoneme (l/igh/t contains one graph, a trigraph and a graph)

Useful reading

- *Beginning to Read: Thinking and Learning about Print* by Marilyn Jager Adams (The MIT Press).
- *Phonics: A Complete Sythentic Programme* and *All New 100 Literacy Hours, Year R* by Wendy Jolliffe (Scholastic Ltd)
- *Independent Review of the Teaching of Early Reading, Final Report* by Jim Rose (DfES, Ref: 0201-2006DOC-EN)

You Can... **Be a good listener**

Being an attentive listener is an essential skill for learning. It is important to teach and model for children what this skill consists of and then to provide plenty of practice in different contexts in order to aid its development. Make sure you provide clear feedback to children on their listening, ensuring you are being specific rather than just saying 'good listening'. This skill will be linked to children's growing ability to concentrate for increasing lengths of time.

Thinking points

● Ask the children what they think good listening is.

● Prompt the children to think about the kinds of things they listen to every day, for example, you, the radio, the TV, their friends, parents/carers and so on. Think about the ways in which you can explain what constitutes good and bad listening.

● Have the children ever been in a situation where they felt that they have not been listened to properly? How did this make them feel? Discuss this with the children.

● Explain why it is important to listen to others when they are speaking.

Tips, ideas and activities

● Role play what poor listening looks like. Do this by:
  ● Asking another adult in the classroom to tell you about an event, such as what they did during the school holidays.
  ● As they talk, demonstrate lack of eye contact by looking around the room. Fidget with your shoes/items of clothing, play with your hair, yawn, face away from the speaker, and so on.
  ● Then ask the children to identify the key things that demonstrated bad listening.

● Use Punch and Judy puppets to re-enact poor listening. If you model this first, then provide puppets and a 'theatre' so children can explore their own versions. Choose children to share their puppet play of poor listening with the class.

● Role play good listening. Once you have explored poor listening, it is important to demonstrate the opposite. You may like to choose two children to show this to the class. As one talks the other listens and shows the particular aspects you have identified, such as 'good eye contact', 'sitting still' and 'not talking until the speaker has finished'.

● Stories related to listening can also be helpful. The best ones are those you tell that incorporate the names of children in the class. Create a story around the theme of a child who does not listen to instructions (such as remembering to hold an adult's hand when in a busy place) with negative results (such as getting lost). Make sure that there is happy ending – you may need to select the child's name with sensitivity – and that the child knows to listen carefully next time!

● Create a poster and display it in the classroom to remind children what good listening should look like.

● Have awards, such as stickers or certificates that say 'good listener' or 'listener of the day'.

You Can... **Help children hear sounds all around**

Before children can begin to learn a systematic phonics programme, it is necessary to ensure that they are able to hear and discriminate between individual sounds. The first step is to use everyday sounds and to have plenty of fun playing games to ensure that they can identify these sounds. The skill of discrimination is related to children's developing vocabulary (they must learn the appropriate nouns associated with sounds), and is also related to the ability to hear degrees, for example of volume or pitch. You will, therefore, need to bear in mind both the physiological ability to hear accurately and also the cognitive ability to name the sound and associate it with the noise it makes.

Thinking points

• We should not assume that children will have the ability to discriminate between individual sounds. We need to teach this discrimination to children and assess their ability in this area as a first step to developing phonological awareness.

• Are you and your colleagues aware of 'glue ear'? This affects hearing and can inhibit the learning progress for children. You may need to suggest to some parents that their children have a hearing test.

• Remember to keep activities fun and only expect very young children to sit and concentrate for short periods.

Tips, ideas and activities

• Gather a range of taped sounds from the environment, such as the washing machine spinning, an alarm clock, a phone ringing, a car starting or birds singing. You can use these in a variety of ways:
  - Play individual sounds to a group or class of children and ask them to identify the sounds to a partner.
  - Have a set of pictures to match the sounds and display the pictures, either on the whiteboard or easel at the front of the class, or on individual 'lotto' boards. As you play each sound, children point to the corresponding picture.
  - Make up a story that can incorporate the sounds on the tape. Pause at appropriate times and play the sounds.

• Use musical instruments to help discriminate volume and pitch. For example:
  - Use a xylophone on which you play very low notes and very high notes. Demonstrate the difference several times before asking children to tell you 'low' or 'high' without assistance.
  - Use a drum to demonstrate volume by playing a loud sound and a soft sound. Ask children to close their eyes and make a different gesture for loud or soft (such as, 'Put your finger on your lips if it is soft. Put your hands over your ears if it is loud.')

• Incorporate sounds into play activities, for example:
  - Small-world toys such as farm animals and zoo animals can be used in conjunction with making the animal noises.
  - Set up a role-play area that would naturally include plenty of different noises, such as a supermarket or train station. You could also have a play microphone for the children to make announcements.

You Can... **Have fun with nursery rhymes**

The ability to hear clearly and distinguish between individual sounds is crucial for the teaching of phonics, and this is also supported by work on rhyme. Children need to be able to hear and spot rhyming words and then also generate their own rhymes. Ensuring that children are familiar with a range of nursery rhymes is an essential part of teaching phonological awareness.

Thinking points

● How often do you share nursery rhymes with the children? Do you have a variety of nursery rhyme tapes and books?

● Do you have a listening area set up with tapes and books of rhymes for the children to explore independently? This can help boost their confidence and learning progress.

● Think about how you can include rhyming as part of your normal everyday activities, such as quick asides to the children. For example:

Hannah Broughton, Hannah Broughton, where are you, where are you?

Here you are, here you are, how do you do!

● Think about how you can link rhymes to a range of activities, such as painting characters from rhymes, re-enacting and singing rhymes such as the 'Grand Old Duke of York'.

Tips, ideas and activities

● Play 'Spot the rhyme'. Say a nursery rhyme together and emphasise the rhyming words. As the children get to know the rhyme, pause for them to provide the rhyming word.

● Have fun with alternative rhymes. See, for example, *Nonsense Nursery Rhymes* by Richard Edwards and Chris Fisher (Oxford University Press). You may also like to create your own alternatives by creating rhyming couplets, for example, 'Humpty Dumpty sat on a log, Humpty Dumpty saw a frog.'

● Create a class book of favourite rhymes.

● Sequence a rhyme using pictures to represent each line. For example, for 'Baa, Baa, Black Sheep', you would create cards showing a black sheep, three bags of wool, a bag of wool next to an important-looking man, and so on. Copy, laminate and then cut up into individual pictures. Support the children to put the pictures in the correct order. This can be done either on a washing line or by providing different pictures to a number of children and then asking them to stand in a line in the correct sequence.

● Involve parents in rhyming activities. Send copies of nursery rhymes home and ask parents to practise with their children, emphasising the rhyming words.

● Provide a range of props and appropriate items of clothing so that children can dress up as famous nursery rhyme characters. Encourage them to re-enact and role play rhymes.

You Can... Share rhymes from different cultures

The importance of being exposed to a range of rhymes is well established as a key aspect of developing phonological awareness. It is also important to ensure that when sharing rhymes with children you include those from different cultures in order to encourage all children to participate, regardless of their home background or culture. Involving parents is also vital to highlight the importance of rhyme and to discover any rhymes that are shared at home.

Thinking points

● Look at your resources. Do you have plenty have rhymes from other cultures either on tapes or in books?

● Have fun reading a range of multicultural rhymes to children (see examples on this page). Do this with plenty of expression and emphasise the rhythm and rhyming words.

● Ensure that you explain unusual words to the children, such as 'mosquito', and also point out whether any rhyming words are nonsense words.

● Remember that frequent repetition of a range of rhymes will help children to remember them. You may wish to include regular short 'rhyme times' during each day.

● Talk to the children about different cultures and their understanding of these. Link the rhymes with the cultures, for example, Chinese rhymes when discussing Chinese New Year, or rhymes from India and Pakistan when talking about celebrating Divali.

● Encourage actions to support the learning of rhymes and to emphasise the rhythm.

Tips, ideas and activities

● Share examples of rhymes from different cultures. For example, see *No Hickory, No Dickory, No Dock* by John Agard and Grace Nichols (Puffin), which is a collection of Caribbean nursery rhymes including the two shown below.

● Create rhyming boxes or bags in a similar way to 'Storysacks' in which you put a range of pictures or objects related to specific rhymes. Share these with children to encourage them to recall the rhyme or match objects that rhyme.

● Use the interactive whiteboard to involve the children in work on rhyme. You could include a range of games such as matching pictures of rhyming words. A variety of ideas for games can be found on the Internet. Develop this idea to include multicultural rhymes.

● Provide materials so that the children can paint or draw characters from rhymes, such as the mosquito in 'Mosquito', and display them next to a copy of the rhyme.

● For rhymes such as 'Abna Babna', which are counting out rhymes, model the way you count out people or objects at the same time as reciting the rhyme.

● Action rhymes will also encourage children's participation.

Mosquito
Mosquito one
Mosquito two
Mosquito jump
In de old man shoe.

Traditional

Abna Babna
Abna Babna
Lady-Snee
Ocean potion
Sugar and tea
Potato roast
And English toast
Out goes she.
(Point to a child or toy. Say the rhyme again until only one child or toy is left.)

Traditional

You Can... **Spot the rhyme**

Once children have had plenty of exposure to rhyme and are able to take part in reciting rhymes, the next step is to ensure that they are able to identify the rhyming words. This is a key step in work on rhyme and is a necessary pre-requisite to children being able to generate their own rhymes or find rhyming words. This can be done in plenty of fun ways using games and songs. Singing is particularly useful in helping develop the aural discrimination of rhyming words.

Thinking points

● When sharing familiar rhymes with the children, try pausing at the rhyming word and encouraging the children to suggest the word that fits.

● An excellent source of suitable rhymes is *This Little Puffin* compiled by Elizabeth Matterson (Penguin), a well-known text for those working with very young children.

● If you are working with older children who need support with hearing rhymes, then limericks or other nonsense rhymes can be a fun way of developing this. See *Michael Rosen's Book of Nonsense* (MacDonald Young).

● A large range of stories for young children are written in rhyming text, such as *The Gruffalo* by Julia Donaldson and Axel Scheffler (Macmillan Children's Books), *Each Peach Pear Plum* by Janet and Allan Alhberg (Puffin) and *It's the Bear!* by Jez Alborough (Walker Books). Have fun with a range of these to encourage children's identification of rhyme.

Tips, ideas and activities

● Rhymes that encourage actions and have accompanying tunes are particularly useful. Well-known favourites that encourage actions are 'Oats and Beans and Barley Grow' or 'When All the Cows Were Sleeping'. The aim is for the children to make the appropriate actions as the rhyming words are spoken. Develop a range that you regularly share with the children.

● Finger rhymes can be fun to share with young children and can support their awareness of the rhyming words. Favourites include 'Two Little Dicky-birds', 'Wind the Bobbin Up' or 'One Finger, One Thumb, Keep Moving'.

● Incorporate role play and story with rhyme. One good example is 'Miss Polly Had a Dolly'. Recite the rhyme encouraging the children to do the actions.

● The use of an interactive whiteboard can support work on rhyme. Try displaying one line of a rhyme at a time and see if the children can say the next line before you display it. For young children who will not be able to read the text, include some graphics to represent the rhyming words.

You Can... **Make up rhymes**

Once children have been able to distinguish rhyming words, the next step is to help them generate rhymes. This clearly demonstrates their ability to hear rhymes and the emerging process of being able to manipulate units of sound. This can be supported in a range of fun ways, including games, songs, and rhyming words for everyday actions. Creating alternative rhymes to well-known nursery rhymes is perhaps the easiest way for children to begin.

Thinking points

● Do you include making up rhymes and jingles as part of your daily activities? If you make these fun the children will be encouraged to make up their own rhymes. For example: 'We are going to play, we'll have fun today.'

● Give children plenty of opportunities to engage in rhyming activities through a wide selection of rhyming books, tapes and games including computer games. Do you have enough of these resources? Do they reflect a variety?

● Think about the ways in which you can assess the children's ability to generate rhymes. For example, one way could be to work with small groups or individual children and ask them which is the odd one out, for example 'cat, hat and dish'.

Tips, ideas and activities

● Begin with oral work substituting well-known rhymes with alternatives, for example 'The Grand Old Duke of York, who used a great big fork'. Start by saying the traditional rhyme to remind the children, and in the case of this rhyme have fun acting it out by marching 'up the hill', and so on. You could build up a range of these either on tape or as a class book you make with the children.

● Have fun establishing passwords in order to go in a certain area of the classroom. For example, the children have to tell you a word that rhymes with 'log'.

● Use interactive whiteboard activities that have initial words already provided, plus a range of possible rhyming words accompanied with pictures, for children to drag and drop into the appropriate slot.

● Draw a picture of an object and then ask the children to draw a rhyming picture, for example, fox and box.

● Use a big book containing rhymes and blank out the rhyming words using Blu-Tack or a sticky note. Then ask the children, as you read the rhyme, to tell you the missing word.

● Use a rhyming story such as *Each Peach Pear Plum* by Janet and Alan Ahlberg (Puffin). Read it together and stop at a rhyming word for the children to supply.

● Have a range of sentences, such as 'I went to bed and bumped my ...' or 'The shed was painted ...' and ask the children to help you supply the missing word.

● Collect a range of pictures of objects that rhyme and ask children to match them. These can be used for a range of games, such as snap or pelmanism (pairs game).

You Can... **Spot the word**

For young children, knowing that the continuous stream of speech they hear is made up of individual words is a complex process, but it is a key part of developing phonological awareness. This also includes understanding that printed text represents the spoken word – an essential element of early reading. The underlying principle is that children are first of all able to develop awareness of larger units of sound, and then go on to break these down into smaller units so that work on individual phonemes can begin.

Thinking points

● Can you help children to discriminate individual words by playing a range of games? For example, have words printed on cards and placed in plastic hoops around the outdoor area, then ask the children to hop onto a word.

● When talking to the children, can you say simple sentences slowly, emphasising each individual word? Use alliteration, such as 'Harry is happy', as this can also help. With children sitting in a circle, encourage them to hold up a finger for each word, or tap each word, for further emphasis.

● Can you find a range of resources that repeat the same word and display these or use with an interactive whiteboard?

● Can you have fun with tongue twisters, such as 'Betty Botter bought some butter' (see page 17).

Tips, ideas and activities

● Poems that contain repetition of the same word can be particularly useful to identify individual words. Try 'Red Rag Rabbit' (shown below).

● Using poems that repeat the same word, children can carry out an action, such as touching their ear, every time they hear a specific word. Another good example of a poem for this is 'A Busy Day' by Michael Rosen (in *A Very First Poetry Book* compiled by John Foster, Oxford University Press) which continually repeats the word 'pop'.

● Using enlarged texts, such as big books or texts on the interactive whiteboard, read together with the children and use a pointer to emphasise the individual words. Once children are able to read the text, they can also enjoy being the 'teacher' and using the pointer. This can act as a very good method of assessment for children who are not able to identify individual words.

● Use the interactive whiteboard to highlight certain words in colour, particularly when one word is repeated. This, alongside emphasis as you read, can support the discrimination of words.

Red Rag Rabbit

Red rag rabbit
    had a red rag rug
that he took to bed
    to keep him snug.

Along came Ted
    and gave a tug
at red rag rabbit's
    red rag rug.

'Stop it, Ted,'
    rag rabbit said,
'It's my rag rug
    that I take to bed.'

Red rag rabbit
    gave Ted a hug,
Here's a tip top toy
    With a string to tug.'

Now Ted had a toy
    with a string to tug,
he didn't want
    red rabbit's rug.

So red rag rabbit
    took his rug to bed
and said, 'Night, night,'
    to his old pal Ted.

Celia Warren

You Can... **Hear syllables**

The process of achieving phonological awareness begins with understanding larger units of sound and then progresses to smaller ones. Once children can distinguish sounds around them and can hear and generate rhymes and individual words, they can then begin to split words into syllables. This is an important step before working on individual phonemes. Work on syllables is accompanied by helping children to 'hear the beat', with links to musical training. Ensuring plenty of practice in a range of ways is the key to achieving the ability to distinguish syllables in words.

Thinking points

● Dividing words into syllables is an important step towards further divisions into phonemes. Think about how you can explain the concept of syllables to the children. For example, in order to be sure how many syllables there are in a word, you may like to share with the children that if you place your hand flat horizontally beneath your chin and say a word. The number of times your chin drops (equivalent to the number of vowel phonemes in the word) denotes the number of syllables. Try this with a multi-syllabic word, such as television = four syllables).

● Alternatively, when you say a word or phrase, clap the syllables at the same time, such as 'dinner time'.

● How can you assess whether children are grasping the idea of syllables? Ensure assessment is ongoing so that any children encountering difficulties with this can have more practice. It may be necessary to reinforce earlier work, such as identifying rhymes, before progressing further.

Tips, ideas and activities

● Play 'My turn, your turn'. You clap or beat the syllables in words and the children copy you.

● Regularly include opportunities for beating/tapping of names, with the children in a circle and taking turns. You may like to incorporate musical instruments, such as tapping a drum, which can be passed round for the children to sound out their names. Have fun tapping names yourself (such as 'La/rry To/tter') for children to guess whose name you are tapping. You will probably need to restrict this to names from the class or tell them it is a favourite character and provide clues.

● Using musical instruments, maintain a syllable pattern. Give a group of children instruments, such a xylophones and drums, and ask them to repeat the pattern you make at the same time as you say a string of words, for example, 'bread and butter'.

● When items are brought in to 'show', children can beat out the syllables, for example, con/ker, ye/llow/ flow/er.

● Show the class or group a number of objects you have in a box. Now ask one child to choose an object from the selection, but not to tell the others which. The child then claps the corresponding number of syllables and the rest of the group has to guess the chosen object.

● Play 'What did you eat today?' Model the reply, saying, 'For breakfast I had...' and then tap out the syllables for the children to guess, for example, corn/flakes. With the children in a circle, each child is asked to tap out what they had and everyone guesses.

You Can... **Learn the alphabet**

Knowing the alphabet, alongside learning the letter names, is a further essential prerequisite to work on phonics. There has been confusion in the past over whether to teach letter names or sounds, and whether the alphabet is important. However, research shows us that alphabetic knowledge is a powerful predictor of later reading success.

Thinking points

● There are two linked skills here: one of recalling the sequence of the letters, and the other of learning the names of all the letters.

● Singing can significantly improve the memory of sequences such as the alphabet. This should be a fun activity, with actions and song to help the recall. This can then be used as a vital tool in knowing the alphabet sequence and the names of the letters.

● Linking the alphabet to the children's names can help, as their names are particularly meaningful to them and also usually the first letters they learn.

● Computer games can also support alphabet knowledge, but check carefully that they are not American versions and that the objects actually correspond to the letters. There are some commercial versions that are incorrect!

● Learning the alphabet requires plenty of practice so that the sequence becomes automatic in time. As adults, we often need to repeat letters in sequence to check alphabetical order.

Tips, ideas and activities

● Learn an alphabet song with the children. The most well known is sung to the tune of 'Twinkle, twinkle little star'. You may also have some commercial tapes of alphabet songs to share with the children.

● Play with 'Alphaboxes', a number of boxes each marked with a different letter of the alphabet. You will need a number of pictures representing different letters of the alphabet. Ask children to work with you or another adult to put each picture in the correct box.

● Alphabet rhymes are another common way of learning the alphabet. For example:

M is for monkey, man and moon
(bend and swing arms like a monkey)
N is for nest, net and noon
(pretend to hold a net and catch things)
O is for octopus, orange, ox and odd
(bend and wave arms around like an octopus)
P is for paper, pen and pea pod
(pretend to write with a pen)

These should be learned in a fun way with accompanying actions. It will require constant repetition for the children to become fully familiar with them.

● Hang large letters of the alphabet onto a washing line. Collect a selection of pictures that represent each letter and ask the children to help you place them on the line.

● Use either commercial alphabet jigsaws or pictures for each letter and help children to put the puzzles together correctly.

● Share alphabet books with the children. For example, *The Absolutely Brilliant Crazy Party* by Wendy Body (Pelican) includes alliterative sentences for each letter and a range of pictures of objects beginning with that letter on each page.

● Create your own alphabet frieze with the children by asking them to paint or draw different objects for each letter.

You Can... **Learn letter names**

The importance of learning the names of the letters as well as the sounds is often misunderstood. Children can learn that a letter has a name as well as the sound it makes. Knowing the names of the letters helps with learning the alphabet and gives clarity when distinguishing letters from phonemes, as when learning that one letter can represent several phonemes (for example, 's' in 'sun' and 'treasure'). This also helps later when identifying letters for spelling words.

Thinking points

● Children are well accustomed to letter names in their everyday lives, for example from well-known brand names, therefore we can build on this knowledge to help them know the names of all letters.

● The identification of upper- and lower-case letters is also important. Relating this concept to children's names and talking about the importance shown by the use of upper case letters can help.

● Identifying letters regardless of font is also important, particularly with lower-case letters, where some, like 'a', can vary quite significantly.

● Work on letter names will go alongside work on the alphabet. Alphabet songs and rhymes all use the letter names, therefore teaching of both will be simultaneous.

Tips, ideas and activities

● Play a variety of alphabet matching games that require cards of all letters of the alphabet (one set for upper-case letters and one for lower-case letters). Ask the children to match lower- to upper-case letters spread on a large table. Alternatively, hang either the upper- or lower-case letters on a washing line and ask the children to peg the corresponding lower- or upper-case letters.

● Play 'Hunt the letter' by providing pages from magazines or comics. Give children several letters and ask them to highlight or ring the same letter when they see it on the pages. A similar activity can be done on the interactive whiteboard with an extract of text.

● Make a letter frieze by collecting together examples of letters in different fonts and sizes. You can ask the children to collect these from a variety of newspapers and magazines.

● Play 'Letters all around'. Accompany the children on 'print walks' around the school, setting or in the immediate environment. Giving them a camera and taking a range of photographs that are then displayed in the classroom can clearly show how we are surrounded by print.

● Letter scrapbooks can also be made by children, where they cut out letters and stick them onto the appropriate page in their books, one letter per page. This is an activity that parents can be encouraged to help with and continue at home.

● Diagnostic assessment activities should be incorporated that clearly identify children who are having difficulties. Use sets of upper- and lower-case letters for children to match and then ask them to tell you the letter name. Keep a record of the children's success.

You Can... **Hear initial phonemes**

The final step in developing phonological awareness is to be able to hear initial sounds (phonemes) in words. The process then moves on to 'phonemic awareness' where the mapping of phonemes (sounds) to graphemes (letters and letter combinations) is taught. First children need to hear and distinguish the beginning sounds in words. The prime way of assisting this is through the use of alliteration, where sentences consist of words that nearly all begin with the same sound, such as 'super sentences sound silly'.

Thinking points

● As this stage is about hearing and identifying initial phonemes, the emphasis is on plenty of oral work with a stress on specific sounds.

● You will need to select different sounds, beginning with those that are easiest to distinguish, such as 's', 'g', 't', 'c'.

● Ensure you note children who are having difficulty hearing and saying the sound correctly. For more guidance on pronunciation see page 19. It is important to ensure that your own pronunciation is correct, avoiding 'uh' as in 'buh', 'muh' an so on.

● At this point, you are not beginning a systematic teaching of all phonemes, so you do not need to work through all the initial sounds. For guidance on this see page 22.

● The use of names of children in the class to create alliterative phrases will also help engage the children.

Tips, ideas and activities

● Rhymes that use alliteration can be fun to share with children as with the example of 'Betty Botter' (shown below). Once you have shared similar examples with the children, go on to make up some and try to include the names of children in the class.

● Silly sentences are an extension of alliteration. The idea is to make the sentences very silly and lots of fun. for example, 'Susan sips silly sausages.'

● 'I spy' games rely on children being able to identify initial phonemes in words. Incorporate this game at various times using the initial sound (phoneme) of the word rather than the letter name, for example, 'I spy with my little eye something beginning with /b/'.

> **Betty Botter**
> Betty Botter bought some butter,
> but, she said, the butter's bitter;
> if I put it in my batter
> it will make my batter bitter,
> but a bit of better butter
> will make my batter better.
> So she bought a bit of butter
> better than her bitter butter,
> and she put it in her batter
> and the batter was not bitter.
> So 'twas better Betty Botter
> bought a bit of better butter.

● Play 'Fishing for phonemes'. This is a game where a range of objects (or pictures of objects) beginning with one or two selected sounds, are placed in a box. Children take turns to 'fish' – take an object – saying, 'I am fishing for phonemes beginning with…'

● The 'Yes/no game' requires 'yes' and 'no' to be written on cards and placed in two different corners of the room. You then say a string of words that begin with the chosen letter and ask the children to point to 'yes' if they think you are correct. Later, intersperse a few words that do not begin with that letter, and the children should point to 'no'.

● Play 'In or out?' This activity requires a selection of objects, some beginning with a selected phoneme and some not. Children then take turns to sort them into designated sorting hoops or rings.

You Can... **Plan a daily discrete lesson**

The latest guidance from the Primary National Strategy states that it is important to plan a daily discrete phonics lesson as part of a systematic programme for the teaching of phonics. This should be part of a rich literacy environment which provides plenty of opportunities for speaking and listening activities and explores the wonderful wealth of children's literature. Regardless of which phonics programme is used, teachers need to ensure that opportunities are provided for practice and over-learning of phonemes and applying them to reading and writing.

Thinking points

● It is important to have a clear structure to lessons that provides practice in hearing, saying, reading and writing the phonemes.

● Lessons should be short (about 15 to 20 minutes maximum), lively and interactive.

● Lessons should be daily, and opportunities for practice included at other times during the day and in other areas of the curriculum, as appropriate.

● Use multi-sensory techniques that include singing, actions, visual aids, and so on.

● Do children already know an alphabet rhyme or song? If so, can you make links to this?

● Include partner work to encourage maximum interaction amongst pupils and more opportunities to practise.

● Observe children carefully to pick up quickly any who need additional support.

● Can you provide follow-up activities that children can do at home in order to involve parents?

Tips, ideas and activities

● Start the lesson with a fun rhyme or song – an alphabet song is ideal, especially if you include actions and have a visual aid for each letter or a frieze.

● Introduce a new phoneme every day. The emphasis should be on teaching the 44 phonemes and their graphemes quickly so that children are able to apply these skills to their developing literacy skills.

● Each lesson should include revision of those phonemes already taught. This can be done quickly by pointing to letters on a chart and children saying the sounds.

● The use of alliterative phrases when teaching consonant and short vowel phonemes is helpful to reinforce the sounds. For example, for the consonant 'l': 'lick the lemon lolly'. This should be accompanied by an action to aid the memory.

● The order of teaching should be as follows:
   1. Say lots of words that contain the sound (to begin with, in the initial position) so that children can listen to it.
   2. Help them to say the sound, ensuring correct pronunciation.
   3. Read the grapheme that represents the sound.
   4. Finally, children should write the grapheme.
This process helps children apply their phonic knowledge to reading and writing. For guidance, see the photocopiable generic lesson plan on page 56.

● Blending phonemes for reading and segmenting words into phonemes for spelling should begin as soon as children have learned a few phonemes. It is therefore important to introduce short vowel sounds early.

You Can... **Pronounce phonemes correctly**

One of the keys to effective phonics teaching is to enunciate the phonemes correctly and model this for the children. The common mistake is to add the 'uh' sound to phonemes so that 'm' becomes 'muh'. This is adding an additional sound and can create problems when children start to blend the phonemes. A pronunciation chart, see photocopiable page 57, is a valuable aid to this so that practitioners can check their pronunciation.

Thinking points

● Do you enunciate pure sounds? It is important to try and avoid the 'uh' sound. However with some consonants, for example 'b', it is almost impossible to make a completely pure sound. Try to keep the sound as clipped as possible – it does help.

● It is also helpful to be aware that some sounds, mainly consonants, can be stretched:

s, n, m, r, f, l, h, z, v, ng, sh, th/th

This is also the case for the short vowels: a, e, i, o and u.

● Other sounds cannot be stretched:

c, t, p (these should be enunciated without the voice)

d, g, b, j, w, y (these need to be enunciated carefully to avoid 'uh')

● Provide plenty of practice for children, listening carefully for those who need extra help in correct enunciation.

Tips, ideas and activities

● As you introduce a new phoneme, make a special point of checking the correct enunciation and modelling this for the children.

● Explaining the position of the mouth, tongue and teeth as you make the sounds will help.

● For some phonemes, such as 'p', you can explain to the children that it is like blowing a candle out on a cake. Tell them to whisper it (it is actually enunciated without the voice).

● Ensure that children can hear the difference between some phonemes where there is a degree of similarity, for example, with 'b' and 'p' and also 't' and 'd'. Refer to the position of the mouth and the tongue as you make the sounds.

● Encourage plenty of practice, with children working with partners, other adults and yourself. Repeating phonemes around a circle in the style of the 'Chinese whispers' game can be a fun way of practising.

● Where you have concerns, listen to children on a one-to-one basis and note any phonemes they are having difficulty with. Work with other adults in the classroom and also parents to encourage practice of correct enunciation. Note that for some children there may be a particular speech difficulty that needs specialist help. Where this is the case, ensure you talk over any concerns with parents or carers. You may also need to enlist the support of your special educational needs coordinator who will be able to coordinate the support of a speech and language specialist. Talking to a specialist can also provide useful guidance on suitable exercises for those who are experiencing difficulties. It is also possible that problems with hearing can have an impact on a child's ability to hear certain sounds and thus reproduce them. This may therefore be another important aspect to check.

You Can... **Count phonemes accurately**

In order to teach children to be proficient in using phonics for reading and spelling, it is important for teachers to be able to segment words into phonemes accurately. This can often present more difficulties for adults than for children, mainly because of the fact that adults have internalised the spelling patterns of the English language and so, when attempting to segment words, they confuse the spelling and the sounds or phonemes. The key is to be aware of the main pitfalls and to practise frequently before teaching children.

Thinking points

● Ensure that you say the words clearly and slowly. Each distinctive sound represents an individual phoneme, for example, 'brick' = /b/r/i/ck/.

● Be wary of consonant blends where consonant letters placed at the beginning and end of words are blended together but actually consist of separate phonemes. For example, in the word 'strap', we hear five phonemes – /s/t/r/a/p/.

● Remember that when counting phonemes or segmenting words into phonemes, this needs to be based on the sounds. It is best to say the word aloud and not to think of the spelling.

● The international phonetic alphabet, which is found at the front of dictionaries, such as the *Oxford English Dictionary*, can be a very useful tool when there is any confusion identifying individual phonemes.

Tips, ideas and activities

● Play 'Phoneme frames'. Children segment written words into the corresponding phonemes by placing the graphemes in separate boxes. You may like to provide boxes of three, four, five or more 'cells' on a laminated sheet so that children can write on with a dry-wipe pen and then erase for future use. For example, 'splash' would appear as:

● Play 'Phoneme fingers'. Say a word. Ask the children to repeat it and then to count individually, on their fingers, the number of phonemes as they say it. They then show you how many 'phoneme fingers' are in the word. You may also like them to pretend to write the letters on each finger for each phoneme.

● Play 'Phoneme buttons'. Present a written version of the word on an easel or interactive whiteboard and then place 'buttons' or dots underneath each phoneme:

m	oo	n
●	●	●

● The progression of teaching should build from CVC (consonant, vowel, consonant) words (eg 'hat') to CCVC (eg 'slap'), CVCC (eg 'nest'), CCCVC (eg 'splat'), CCVCC (eg 'stand') and multi-syllabic words (eg 'mummy', 'homework'). Ensure when working on CVC words that they do not contain digraphs, for example, 'boy' – which consists of two phonemes /b/oy/, with /oy/ being a vowel digraph (two letters making one sound).

● For further guidance on segmenting words into phonemes, see the *Primary National Strategy: Primary Framework for Literacy and Mathematics, Subject Leader Handbook* (Ref 02009-2006DVD-EN) 'Phonics Subject Knowledge'.

You Can... **Use multi-sensory methods**

By reviewing different methods of teaching phonics, the Rose Report identified the importance of multi-sensory methods. It is recommended that providing simultaneous visual, auditory and kinaesthetic activities can support children's learning. Part of the reason for such a recommendation is the increasing emphasis on providing for a range of learning styles for children (although the research evidence for this is often disputed). Nevertheless, practitioners know from experience that providing different ways to support children's learning through actions, sounds and visual prompts is very successful.

Thinking points

● Are you always consistent in teaching the same actions for a phoneme? You may like to follow the guidance from a particular scheme, for example *Phonics: A Complete Synthetic Programme* by Wendy Jolliffe (Scholastic Ltd).

● Build a stock of pictures that help support each phoneme (/s/ = snake, sand, saw, spider, and so on). Use this to display and for frequent use. For example, when the children revise phonemes taught, as you show a picture, they say the word.

● The use of alliteration can be very helpful in the early phases of teaching phonics with consonants and short vowel sounds, for example, 'snakes on slippery sand'. Frequent repetition of alliterative sentences can ensure that children are able to identify initial phonemes in words.

Tips, ideas and activities

● Either following a specific programme that incorporates multi-sensory teaching, or devising your own, develop actions to accompany each phoneme learned. For example, for the phoneme /f/ say 'five floppy fish flap' and flap your arms like a fish. You will need constant revision of phonemes learned using the alliterative phrase and action each time. This is particularly useful for children who have difficulty recalling phonemes taught.

● Visual prompts should accompany the sound and action. Either use clipart pictures from your computer or download from the internet. Provide several pictures for each phoneme, but ensure that they do depict a word that corresponds to the phoneme. Incorrect examples include 'island' for the short vowel sound /i/ and 'eel' for the short vowel sound /e/.

● Songs, rhymes and raps are also a powerful way of supporting children's learning of phonemes. It is important that the rhymes do not detract from the phoneme children are learning. Some phonics programmes emphasise a character for initial consonant phonemes that can detract from actually learning the phoneme. The long vowel phonemes and the varied ways of writing the same phoneme are particularly difficult for children to learn. For example, the phoneme /ae/ can be written as 'ay' in 'day', 'ai' as in 'sail', 'a' as in 'able', or 'a_e' as in 'cake'. The use of a rap to support has been shown to really help children (see page 26). For example:

'ee', 'ee'	f**ee**l the tr**ee**	**EE** *(say letter names)*
'ow', 'ow'	r**ow** it sl**ow**	**OW**
'oo', 'oo'	r**oo**m on the m**oo**n	**OO**

● For use of magnetic letters and other resources to support multi-sensory teaching, see Chapter 5.

You Can... **Teach initial phonemes**

Teaching initial phonemes is the easiest starting point for young children. This should only begin when children have demonstrated that they have good phonological awareness and are able to hear and discriminate different sounds (as detailed in Chapter 1). It is important to teach a combination of consonants and short vowel sounds so that very early on children are able to blend phonemes into words. The most common phonemes are /s/ /a/ /t/ /p/ /i/ /n/, which can be combined to make a range of words.

Thinking points

● Teaching initial phonemes should very quickly lead to the teaching of consonant vowel consonant (CVC) words due to the importance of ensuring that children learn to blend the phonemes.

● Teaching initial phonemes should progress at a fast pace. The *Primary National Strategy* recommends that in Phase 2 of a systematic programme (Phase 1 concerns developing phonological awareness) children should be introduced to a small selection of common consonants and vowels which they blend together in reading and spelling simple CVC words and that this should last up to six weeks.

● At this stage, teaching initial phonemes will typically start with group or class work and, after careful observation, provision of additional support for individual children where necessary. Identifying children who are unsure of any phonemes at this stage is essential in order to provide effective early intervention.

Tips, ideas and activities

● When teaching each phoneme, ensure that you clearly show the link between hearing the sound, reading the corresponding grapheme and writing it. To do this, the following sequence will provide valuable reinforcement:

Hear it: Say a range of words containing the phoneme in the initial position and then children identify the phoneme. Reinforce with an alliterative phrase and an appropriate action.

Say it: Reinforce correct pronunciation of the sound and ask children to practise saying it several times. Use robot talk and say several words containing the phoneme taught, asking the children to blend the phonemes into words.

Read it: Show a card of the grapheme and say the phoneme. Combine it with other phonemes taught in order to blend as soon as possible.

Write it: Say the phoneme again and ask the children to write the letter. Provide cues for letter formation and apply to words as soon as possible.

● Phonic games can be a useful reinforcement of phonemes taught. A range of these are found in *Progression in Phonics* (DfES, 1999) and *Playing with Sounds* (DfES, 2004). See also page 31.

● One of the keys to effective phonics teaching is to provide constant over-learning. This is achieved by quickly revisiting recent phonemes taught at the beginning of a lesson, and then progressing to a new phoneme. Teaching a new phoneme each day and then having a revision day, for instance every fifth day, is also useful.

● Accurate assessment of pupils' understanding is crucial. This can be supported by on-going formative assessment using, for example, 'show me' activities such as writing corresponding graphemes on a mini-whiteboard and showing you. In addition, you will need to regularly assess individual children to check their growing understanding.

You Can... **Teach medial and final phonemes**

Once children have begun to learn some initial phonemes it is very important that they learn to identify phonemes in different positions in words. This is a key part of the skill of blending phonemes for reading. The early introduction of CVC words will help this process, but for some children the ability to identify phonemes in final positions is more difficult than in the initial position; even more so for medial phonemes. Important aspects that support children concern frequent exposure to hearing phonemes in different positions and the ability to talk in robot talk.

Thinking points

● As soon as you have taught a few consonant and vowel phonemes (/s/ /a/ /t/ /p/ /i/ /n/) begin work on blending three-letter words (CVC). You will need to ensure that you model this clearly with careful articulation of sounds. Closely linked to this is the use of robot talk, where each phoneme is said individually. (For more guidance on this, see page 36.)

● Although it is important that children can hear phonemes in different positions in words, it must be borne in mind that this should not delay the process of teaching all 44 phonemes. If this is taught concurrently with introducing common consonants and short vowels through CVC words, then it will not cause unnecessary delays.

Tips, ideas and activities

● The use of a puppet that can't hear final (or medial) phonemes in words can support this process in a fun way. The puppet can try to say the name of a range of objects, but does so incorrectly. For example, instead of 'pat', the puppet says 'pad', or for medial phonemes the puppet says 'pan' instead of 'pin', and so on. The children have to help to correct the puppet each time. This is also found in the *Progression in Phonics* 'Croaker' materials related to final phonemes (DfES, 1999).

● Play 'Spot the middle phoneme'. Here you supply some initial and final phonemes for words but the children have to suggest a medial phoneme to make a word, for example:

s _ n   t _ p   n _ p   a _ t   p _ t   s _ t

● Play 'Make a word'. The aim of this activity is to provide some separate letters on cards, from which children have to see if they can make words. This will start with simple CVC words and can progress to CCVC and CVCC words, and so on as appropriate:
   ● Step 1: For phonemes /s/ /a/ /t/ /p/ /i/ /n/, select three phonemes to make CVC words and place them in separate bags (/s/ /a/ /t/ in one bag and /p/ /i/ /n/ in the other).
   ● Step 2: Use the same technique for CCVC words, as in 'clap', and CVCC words, as in 'vest'. Phonemes selected will depend on those taught.
   ● Step 3: Include some digraphs (as in '**ch**ef') and trigraphs (as in 'wa**tch**') and follow the same procedure.

● Regularly use magnetic letters to support blending phonics to make words.

You Can... **Teach consonant blends**

Ensuring that children are able to clearly distinguish individual phonemes where consonants are blended together is important for two reasons: firstly for determining the number of phonemes in a word, and secondly for being able to spell the word correctly. Again this should be taught as part of work on teaching all 44 phonemes. It is not a separate stage that requires a lengthy period of teaching. Consonant blends can be introduced after children have learned some common consonants and short vowel phonemes.

Thinking points

● Ensure that before you teach words containing consonant blends, you yourself can distinguish the individual phonemes. Say a word slowly, particularly if it contains a consonant blend, and if you can distinguish separate sounds ('strap' = /s/t/r/a/p/, slip = /s/l/i/p/), then they are individual phonemes. By contrast, in the word 'ship', it is impossible to separate 's' and 'h': they are one phoneme /sh/ – a digraph. Confusion may also occur with words that contain consonant blends at the end of the word. For example, 'duck' does not contain a consonant blend, as 'ck' is a digraph where two letters make one sound. As before, the test is whether the sounds can be separated. In 'duck' /d/u/ck/, it is not possible to separate /ck/ – it is one phoneme.

● The guidance from the *Primary National Strategy* states that this should be Phase 4, 'Teaching children to read and spell words containing adjacent consonants', which follows from teaching one grapheme for each of the 44 phonemes. However, as this will include the long vowel phonemes, you may wish to introduce some CCVC (eg 'flap') and CVCC (eg 'best') words earlier, ensuring you do not confuse digraphs and blends as you do so.

Tips, ideas and activities

● Playing 'Phoneme fingers' (see page 20) is particularly useful for ensuring that children can hear each phoneme in words containing consonants blends. Ensure that when you introduce these you do not include digraphs which would cause confusion. Examples of suitable words include:

CCVC: blog, clap, drip, flip, grin, smug, trip, plug
CVCC: best, mast, tend

● Play 'Phoneme frames' (again, as explained on page 20), for example: | s | t | a | m | p |

Ensure you model this process on an easel or interactive whiteboard and then provide opportunities for children to practise, for example, in pairs using mini-whiteboards divided into squares, or provide blank boxes on laminated paper and use dry-wipe pens.

● Practise reading decodable sentences that contain consonant blends with the children, for example, by including some in text on the interactive whiteboard. This will need to include words that the children are able to decode (and have been taught so far), as per the example below:

Stop, stop! See the big hen. It is sad. Go and help. It is stuck in the gap. Can you get it?

While such text will seem rather boring, it makes useful practice of decoding and it should not mean that a wealth of children's literature cannot still be explored with children!

You Can... **Teach digraphs and trigraphs**

It is important to have a clear understanding that, in the English language, a different number of letters can denote one phoneme (the grapheme). It is possible to have one letter making one phoneme (a graph), such as in the word 'fig' where there are three graphs (/f/i/g/). However, it is also possible to have two letters representing the phoneme (a digraph), as at the end of 'fish' (/f/i/sh/), or three letters representing one phoneme (a trigraph), as in the middle of the word 'light' (/l/igh/t/). Occasionally, there may be four letters representing one phoneme as in 'eight' (/eigh/t/). The relative frequency of digraphs and trigraphs make it important that these are clearly taught.

Thinking points

● Confusion when counting phonemes is often due to a lack of knowledge of digraphs and trigraphs. The following words are not CVC words – rather, they contain a consonant and a vowel digraph:

boy = /b/oy/
cow = /c/ow/
car = /c/ar/
day = /d/ay/
new = /n/ew/

● Confusion may also arise from the different ways of representing a given phoneme with vowel digraphs. For example, the phoneme /ae/ can be represented as 'ay' in 'day', 'ai' in 'tail', 'a' in 'able', or 'a_e' in 'cake'. For further guidance on this see page 26. The knowledge that the position of the vowel in the word can affect the spelling can be helpful, so for example, /ae/ is commonly written as 'a_e' and 'ai' in the beginning and middle of the word and 'ay' at the end of a word.

Tips, ideas and activities

● Common consonant digraphs that are taught first are /sh/ and /ch/ plus /th/ (unvoiced, as in 'thin') and /th/ (voiced, as in 'then'). These can be taught in the same way as other consonants as part of a systematic programme.

● Other consonant digraphs are best taught accompanied by learning rules regarding their use, for example:
  - After a short vowel, consonants are often doubled. For example, words end in 'ss' instead of 's' ('miss'), 'ff' instead of 'f' ('tiff'), 'll' instead of 'l' ('will'), and 'zz' instead of 'z' ('buzz').
  - After a short vowel, words end in 'ck' instead of 'k' ('duck').
  - In words of two syllables, medial consonants are doubled, for example, 'bb' in 'rabbit', 'dd' in 'puddle', 'mm' in 'hammer', 'ff' in 'coffee', 'rr' in 'cherry', and 'tt' in 'letter'.

● Vowel digraphs need to be taught systematically, focusing on the most common spelling of the digraph to begin with and then gradually building a chart to show the alternative spellings (for further guidance see page 26).

● Trigraphs are also common in English. Begin by teaching the consonant trigraphs, of which there are not many:
  'dge' – in 'bridge'
  'tch' – in 'watch'
There are a large number of vowel trigraphs, for example:
  'igh' – in 'light'
  'air' – in 'hair'
  'ear' – in 'fear'
For a complete list of these, see photocopiable page 58. Ensure that these are taught systematically. Due to the complexity of these phonemes, the use of multi-sensory methods, including raps, can be very helpful.

You Can... **Teach long vowel phonemes**

Long vowel phonemes are the most complex aspect of teaching phonics and in the past have often not been taught systematically and not to young children. Without them, however, the ability to decode text using phonics is severely limited. It is important to help children to learn all 20 vowel phonemes. Using multi-sensory methods can make this achievable for young children, and can be accompanied by the teaching of a range of spelling rules.

Thinking points

● Long vowel phonemes need systematic teaching and opportunities for over-learning. This can be done each day and built upon as you learn a new phoneme. If you learn using raps, as suggested below right, this can be a fun way of starting each phonics session.

● It is important for children to see that long vowel phonemes consisting of digraphs or trigraphs are units. They should not attempt to sound out each letter.

● Careful assessment of children's progress is vital to ensure that extra support is provided to those children who need it. See page 54 for guidance on assessing long vowel phonemes.

● Encourage parents to support children, for example, by sending a rhyme or rap home for practice with guidance. It will also be very useful to hold workshops to explain more fully to parents the methods you are using.

Tips, ideas and activities

● Teaching all 20 vowel phonemes is important. The easiest way to approach this is to begin by teaching the five short vowel phonemes (/a/e/i/o/u/) and then work systematically through the remainder. You may decide to teach the most common representation of each of the long vowel phonemes first and then later teach all other ways of spelling the phoneme. The full list is shown as part of the phoneme chart on photocopiable page 58 (most common usages are given first).

● Learning a rap or rhyme for each of these phonemes can be very helpful to support young children, particularly if accompanied by actions. For example:

Say the phoneme twice	Say the rhyme	Say the letter names	Do an action
ee/ee	**F**ee**l** the tr**ee**	E E	Pretend to hug a tree
ea/ea	**H**ea**t** the m**ea**t	E A	Pretend to stir with a spoon

● The use of visual aids can also support learning long vowel phonemes. You may like to make a series of picture cards to fit the rap you create.

You Can... Help children understand that one letter does not always make one sound

Another difficulty with phonics in the English language is the many different ways of representing the same phoneme – in other words, the different spelling choices or graphemes. Children often identify this difficulty early, particularly when they find their names do not conform to the common spelling, for example, 'Chloe' where the common representation is 'c' or 'k' for the phoneme /c/. It is therefore important to teach that one letter does not always make the same sound and that the same phoneme can be written in different ways (as with /f/, which can commonly be written as 'f', 'ff' or 'ph').

Thinking points

● Make use of a chart (see the long vowel section of the phoneme chart on photocopiable page 58) to visually demonstrate the different spelling choices. This is particularly important for the long vowel phonemes.

● Make very explicit when teaching that the same phoneme can be represented in more than one way. For example, /ae/ can be writing as 'a', 'a_e', 'ai', 'ay', with other less common representations: 'ey' (in 'prey') and 'eigh' (in 'weigh'). It is, however, important to focus on the most common ways and gradually add others as appropriate.

● Be particularly aware of spellings of names (first names and surnames) from other cultures which vary from English orthography. Use these as a point of reference for talking about the different ways of spelling the same phoneme.

Tips, ideas and activities

● Play 'How many ways?' Once you have taught a range of different graphemes for a phoneme, see if children can identify how many different ways a particular phoneme can be spelled. You may like to develop this as a game.

● Play 'Match the phoneme and grapheme'. This activity would be ideal for an interactive whiteboard. Have a specific phoneme displayed in the centre of the screen with, as shown below, a selection of correct and incorrect spellings around the edge. The children have to select the correct spellings.

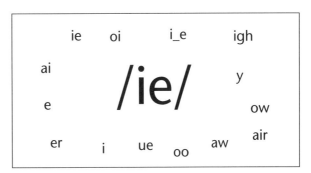

● Develop a mural of names grouped according to phonemes, for example: Phil, Phillippa, Fiona, Freddie. Investigate unusual names and spellings involving parents and members of the community.

● Play 'Which grapheme?' The aim is for children to make the correct spelling choice for a phoneme. This can be done in a variety of ways. Say a word and ask the children to identify the correct grapheme from a selection written on the easel or interactive whiteboard, or on cards.

You Can... Build a chart of phonemes

To support children, it is useful to create a chart of phonemes as you teach each one. Focus on the most common graphemes for each phoneme first, then add those that you feel are most appropriate for the age of the children. The key is to gradually build a chart as you teach each grapheme or representation of the same phoneme. In this way, you can build up a large chart to refer to in the classroom. You may wish to include pictures to represent each phoneme to make the chart both more useful and more attractive. Ensure you use it with the children for constant reference.

Thinking points

● You may wish to create separate charts, one for consonants and short vowel phonemes and a different one for long vowel phonemes. Alternatively, you may wish to create one for consonants and one for all vowels. The chart is a teaching tool. It is therefore important that you use it constantly. See the example chart on photocopiable page 58.

● The example chart gives the most common spelling choice/grapheme for each phoneme first. For example, the phoneme /t/ is most commonly written with the single letter 't'.

● If you put the chart on an interactive whiteboard you may be able to drag and drop particular phonemes and their corresponding graphemes. This will also enable you to manipulate the chart in a variety of ways.

Tips, ideas and activities

● The use of charts is a constant visual reminder of the structure of the language. The chart on photocopiable page 58 is an example of a combined chart for all 44 phonemes divided into consonants and short vowels, and long vowels.

● You may wish to create an outline chart on the wall, arranged in the order in which you propose to teach, with 29 boxes for the 24 consonant phonemes and 5 short vowel phonemes and a further 15 boxes for the long vowel phonemes. As you teach a phoneme and its common spelling, place it on the chart.

● When you teach the long vowel phonemes (see page 26) you may wish to build a separate chart that shows the different graphemes for the same phoneme. As this is the most complex aspect of learning phonics, this can be a very useful tool for reference.

● Ensure that any chart you create is clear for children, using pictures as appropriate. The complex charts used in some schemes can be too difficult for young children. They can, however, be a useful reference tool for teachers.

● You may like to use a chart to play games, such as 'Find the phoneme', where you say a phoneme that has been taught and a child points to it on the chart.

You Can... **Review lessons regularly**

It is very important during a systematic programme of teaching phonics to provide regular review sessions. This not only helps over-learning of phonemes, but also provides opportunities to assess children's progress. The format of these lessons should provide for reinforcement of hearing, saying, reading and writing the sounds and can incorporate some phonic games. Where children are unsure of phonemes, provide opportunities for extra support.

Thinking points

● Schedule review lessons regularly (approximately every five days), keeping careful records of those children who require additional support.

● Look for a variety of ways of reinforcing phonemes taught, including games (see page 31 for suggestions). Make use of an interactive whiteboard and computer games for added reinforcement. Where possible, provide additional practice with reading phonically decodable books (these may also be sent home).

● Do you involve parents with supporting and reinforcing phonemes? You could provide a weekly update of phonic work covered, for example:

> Phonemes taught this week: _____
> Games you can play: _____
> Other ways of supporting at home: _____

This will need to be linked to workshops and briefing sessions so that parents feel confident to help.

● Develop a tracking system for all children to record their growing phonic knowledge (see page 55 for a suggested format).

Tips, ideas and activities
Hear it
● Use cards that display pictures corresponding to the phoneme, such as an apple and an ant for /a/. Say the word for each picture and ask the children to say the word after you. Then ask the children what sound they can hear. Repeat for all letters covered during the week in a brisk, pacy way.

● Play a game for reinforcement. See the suggestions in *Progression in Phonics* (DfES, 1999), *Playing with Sounds* (DfES, 2004) or *Phonics: A Complete Synthetic Programme* by Wendy Jolliffe (Scholastic Ltd, 2006, pp.46–53).

Say it
● Use several words containing the phonemes taught in initial, medial and final position, and say these slowly in robot talk.

● Ask children to talk in robot talk and say words in segments.

Read it
● Using letter cards, quickly show the children ones learned that week and ask them to tell you the sound each makes.

● Select three words for each phoneme taught that week and ask the children to read by blending using robot talk.

Write it
● Provide the children with individual whiteboards and pens. Explain that you are going to say the phoneme and the children will write the letter. Quickly revise all letters taught that week.

● Tell children a word containing a recently taught phoneme. First ask them to tell you how many phonemes are in the word by counting on their fingers and showing you. Then ask them to write the word. Practise for all phonemes taught that week.

● Ask the children to write words using phonemes taught.

● Check children's ability to hear, read and write phonemes taught and provide reinforcement for those who need it.

You Can... **Teach tricky words**

There are a number of words in English that are irregular, for example, 'was' and 'once'. These words have led to a lack of faith in the teaching of phonics for learning to read, because /w/a/s/ pronounced in the way in which we would normally say each of these phonemes will never make 'was'. An understanding of the different spellings of the same phonemes can make this clearer. Nevertheless, for young children it is helpful to learn a small number of words as 'tricky words'. These can be taught as 'sight' words and recognised from the shape and letters.

Thinking points

● Teach only a few words as 'tricky' words and where possible help children to decode most words phonetically. This helps to eliminate the need to memorise a large number of words. Previously, when teaching reading relied on 'look and say' methods, this was the principal way of learning, and whilst those children with good visual memories made progress, those without, particularly children with dyslexia, did not.

● Many 'tricky words' can be decoded once children acquire a thorough knowledge of all 44 phonemes. However, as these are high frequency words, it is helpful to learn some by sight.

● The original *National Literacy Strategy Framework* specifies 45 'sight words' by the end of Reception and a further 150 words between Year 1 and Year 2. However, guidance accompanying the renewed *Primary Framework for Literacy and Mathematics* (2006) states that many of these contain common letter–sound correspondences.

Tips, ideas and activities

● Introduce tricky words gradually once children are able to blend CVC words. Limit the learning of these to two or three per week depending on the children you are teaching. For example:

1. said	are	the
2. come	was	some
3. once	two	want
4. there	your	what
5. where	who	because
6. laugh	people	their
7. would	could	should

Note that 'could', 'would' and 'should' can be taught phonetically alongside teaching the long vowel phoneme /u/ which can be written as 'oo' in 'book', 'u' in 'put', as well as 'ou' in 'could'.

● The use of mnemonics, or sayings, can be helpful in supporting children when learning tricky words. Some mnemonics give a word for each letter:
'said' – '**S**ally **A**nn **i**s **d**izzy'
'because' – '**b**ig **e**lephants **c**an **a**lways **u**se **s**mall **e**xits'
Others focus on problematic parts of the word:
'could', 'would' or 'should' – 'O U lucky duck'

● Point out examples of tricky words during shared and guided reading to support children. It will also be helpful to create a display of them for constant reference. These are sometimes called 'red' words – words that cannot be sounded out – as opposed to 'green' words, which can be. You may like to print them onto red card to display this visually.

● As children learn a greater number of phonemes and the alternative ways of spelling them, you may wish to point out that many tricky words can be sounded out. For example, the word 'said' consists of the phonemes /s/ai/d/, with 'ai' being another spelling choice for the phoneme /e/.

You Can... **Play phonic games**

Games are a very useful way of reinforcing phonic knowledge. Not only are they fun for young children, but they encourage plenty of oral work as well as interaction amongst pupils. Whilst the teaching of phonemes should be accompanied by teaching the correct letter formation, the emphasis when teaching phonics should be on oral work, avoiding the use of worksheets. These can often amount to little more than colouring in and do not help the learning of phonemes.

Thinking points

● Many games can be adapted for teaching a range of phonemes. One such is the 'Yes/no game'. You say a word, and if it begins with a specific phoneme, the children point to a 'yes' sign you have posted in the classroom.

● The *National Literacy Strategy Progression in Phonics* materials (1999) contain a fund of games which can be very useful. In addition, the accompanying photocopiables include some large A4-size letters. These are a very useful resource and it is recommended that you copy and laminate all 26 letters, together with the most common digraphs ('sh', 'ch' and 'th').

● Other resources to collect include objects and pictures that represent initial letter sounds. Puppets can also be useful, either for children to correct (the puppet says it wrongly!) or, if the puppet can only speak in phonemes, for children to blend the phonemes to make a word.

Tips, ideas and activities

● Play the 'Sorting game'. This is useful for reinforcing the teaching of initial phonemes. You will need an assortment of objects that represent the initial sound. For example, for the phoneme /t/: teapot, toy tiger, telephone, tambourine, tape, tissue, toaster. In addition, have some objects that do not begin with the chosen phoneme. Now, using a sorting hoop and with the children sitting in a circle, pass the objects around, preferably one to each child. Children take turns to place the object in the hoop if it begins with /t/ (or whichever phoneme you select).

● Magnetic letters can also be a very useful resource, either using a large magnetic board and letters with the whole class or group of children, or using several smaller sets of letters and boards. Provide a selected number of letters corresponding to the phonemes taught. For example, if you have taught the phonemes /s/ /a/ /t/ /p/ /i/ /n/, give the children two or three of each letter. Then in an allotted time (you may like to use a sand-timer) see how many words they can make.

● Bingo is another popular game with children. It can be used in a variety of ways, however one very useful game is to provide several different game boards, each with approximately six words on that can be phonically decoded by the children. An example board is shown below. This is very useful practice at blending phonemes for reading. Have a set of words yourself and put them to one side as you read each one. Children cross off each word if they can find it on their board and shout 'bingo!' when they have them all crossed off.

net	sad	top
pig	dog	ant

You Can... # Help children blend phonemes for reading

Teaching children to identify phonemes is not sufficient for reading unless the skill of blending them together is taught alongside. In the past this was often left until later. As soon as children know a few phonemes (consonants and short vowels) then this process can begin. As this skill develops, they will be able to blend phonemes in the order in which they occur through a word – and so read it. It is important to make clear that blending and segmenting are reversible processes, the former for reading and the latter for spelling.

Thinking points

● Start early. As soon as a few phonemes are known begin the process of teaching children to blend them together. Continue as you introduce each new phoneme to include blending with other phonemes taught.

● Constant practice will be needed in order to help children move from the rather staccato sounds they make in response to reading letters to blending them together into seamless words. The key to this is to explicitly model blending phonemes into words, ensuring children practise after hearing it. Carefully observe children, where possible using teaching assistants or other adults to help, in order to identify children who may need additional support.

● The process of blending is closely linked to segmenting phonemes, which is required for spelling words. This will therefore link to robot talk – for more guidance on this see page 36.

Tips, ideas and activities

● Oral blending is a vital skill and requires frequent practice. You can do this in a variety of fun ways:
  ○ Passwords. Here children need to tell you a password in order to go out to play, for example. You tell them the constituent phonemes in a word first and they have to whisper the word (the password) to you.
  ○ Use a puppet who you tell the children can only speak in phonemes. The puppet tells the children a word in phonemes, for example /p/l/ay/, and the children have to say the word, 'play', by orally blend the phonemes.

● It is also important for children to be able to read letters (graphemes), say the corresponding phonemes and then blend them into words. Part of this skill requires that children read the graphemes from left to right in the correct order in which they are written in the word. To support, use a pocket chart in which you place several individual letters which will make words (beginning with CVC words), or stick individual graphemes on a board or wall with Blu-Tack. Now use a pointer to highlight the direction of reading the graphemes and to physically demonstrate the process of putting the graphemes/phonemes together.

● Work on blending should be closely linked to segmenting. This is helped by the use of the following strategies within each phonics session:
  ○ Hear it: you say several words that contain the specific phoneme so the children can identify the phoneme.
  ○ Say it: help the children to enunciate the phoneme correctly.
  ○ Read it: read the graphemes, blending phonemes together to make words.
  ○ Write it: you say a phoneme and the children write the corresponding grapheme, followed by saying a word and then segmenting into phonemes and the children write the word.

You Can... **Help children practise blending**

Research has shown that being able to blend phonemes makes a significant difference to learning to read. The Primary National Strategy's survey in 2005 found that there was little teaching of blending in schools. It is important to provide children with plenty of practice in doing this orally, both by reading and not referring to graphemes, then saying the corresponding phonemes and blending them into words. One invaluable way of doing this orally is through the use of robot talk, where the children hear the individual phonemes and then blend them into words.

Thinking points

● Model blending phonemes frequently with the children. You may do this incidentally, for example, pointing out a sign around the school or setting and saying each phoneme before you blend them into a word. You should also regularly plan to spend some time modelling blending phonemes during phonics sessions (see page 34 for guidance).

● Link this to work on segmenting so that children may see these are reversible processes, see particularly the use of robot talk on page 36.

● Integrate work on blending into all practice at reading: in shared reading using enlarged texts or big books, or in guided group sessions. Where appropriate, model blending phonemes for reading using a pointer in order to emphasise the direction of print and letters within a word.

Tips, ideas and activities

● Shared reading is an invaluable tool in demonstrating how to decode texts using phonics, as well as sharing the joy of reading a wide range of texts. In the selection of texts that you choose, there will often be repeated refrains or words that children can decode phonetically. Select some of these and ask the children to say the phonemes in a word with you, then blend them together to make a word.

● Guided reading is another important way of supporting children's ability to build phonemes. Ensure that you have a clear focus for each session which is carefully matched to the children's reading ability. As children begin learning phonics, the use of phonetically decodable books can be useful for practice.

● Another way of supporting children's early attempts at independent reading is through helping them to make their own books. Provide blank A5-size books which you have made by folding a sheet of A4 coloured paper and inserting inside it two white folded A4 pages and then stapling down the left-hand side. You can use these books in the following ways:
  ● Provide a number of words that can be read phonetically from phonemes already taught and ask children to order them into sentences. Supported by an adult or parent, the adult then writes the sentence in the child's book (or later, the child her/himself) for the child to read.
  ● After completing exercises to blend a number of words from phonemes taught, these are put into a sentence through shared reading (by writing on an easel or interactive whiteboard). The sentences are transferred by the teacher or another adult into the child's own book for practice, particularly at home.

You Can... **Play games blending words**

Practising the important skill of blending requires a variety of methods. Games are a fun and motivational way to support this and should be included whenever possible for additional practice. They are particularly useful for practising oral blending of phonemes. Gradually accumulating a bank of games for this purpose provides a key resource. Keep the various resources needed together in a bag or wallet, carefully labelled so a range of adults can access them.

Thinking points

● Include games in review lessons which should be scheduled regularly, for example every five days, for additional practice. Include games at other appropriate times, working with small groups or the whole class.

● For children who show they need further consolidation in learning specific phonemes, you may wish to provide games for a teaching assistant or adult to use with individuals or groups. It is vitally important that you carefully monitor children's progress in order to decide where this is appropriate.

● Provide ideas for games for parents to use at home as reinforcement. Many phonic games require few resources and can be adapted in various ways once the idea is clear.

Tips, ideas and activities

● Play 'Follow that sign!' The idea of this is to create a number of signs that you then place around the setting or classroom, both inside and outside. These will need to be appropriate to the children's phonic knowledge and progress with 'tricky words'. For example:

Sit on the mat!
Stop not here!
Go in the sand.
Tap the drum.
Hop on the mat.

● Play 'Class treasure trail'. Write some clues on cards dotted around the classroom or setting and ask the children to follow the trail. An adult's help will support this, particularly if some words are difficult. This supports positional language well, which is an area many children find complex. Clues could include:

On the rug.   On top of the bench.
Under the desk.   Over the door.

● Computer games are another way of reinforcing phonic knowledge. You may wish to devise your own either using individual computers and encouraging children to work in pairs, or using an interactive whiteboard ensuring that children can reach to drag and drop or manipulate it. For blending phonemes, games could include separate graphemes dotted around the screen and children drag and drop them to make words, which will require them to blend the corresponding phonemes.

● Linking reading (or blending phonemes) to a role-play area can be a powerful incentive. One example could be a café where children are given specific roles (with badges, such as waiter, customer, cook). Provide examples of print such as menus and then, with adult support, help children to read the words by sounding out and blending phonemes, for example, 'ham and chips'.

You Can... **Help children segment words into phonemes for spelling**

Segmentation is the corresponding skill to blending and requires children to segment or divide words into their constituent phonemes. So, for example, in the word 'stand' there are five phonemes: /s/ /t/ /a/ /n/ /d/. In order to be able to write words, children need to apply this process. With constant practice, this becomes automated and children rely on their phonic knowledge for spelling words. This can be problematic at first and will require later work on selecting appropriate spelling choices for phonemes and gradually internalising the orthographic patterns of our language to make the correct choices.

Thinking points

● One of the most powerful ways of teaching segmentation is through the use of robot talk (see page 36). Provide plenty of practice of this in every phonics session or at other appropriate times in the day.

● Incorporate segmenting and blending into every phonics lesson by saying a word and asking children to segment it into phonemes. Then write a word containing phonemes taught on the whiteboard and help children to blend the phonemes to read the word.

Tips, ideas and activities

● In chapter 2, the use of 'phoneme fingers' and 'phoneme buttons' was recommended to support children in counting phonemes accurately (see page 20). Both of these are very useful for teaching children to segment words into the constituent phonemes.

● In shared writing, encourage the children to suggest the phonemes they can hear in a word and then the graphemes that you need to write.

● Encourage children to link reading and writing (blending phonemes and segmenting words into phonemes) by making their own books which contain sentences they can read phonetically. Relate these to their own experiences or interests, either scribing these for the child or encouraging them to write their own sentences.

● Frequently model the process of orally segmenting words and then writing the corresponding graphemes on the whiteboard or easel. Link this to writing items about items and events of particular interest to the children.

● Provide practice at segmenting words and writing the corresponding graphemes using partner work and mini-whiteboards. Read out words that include phonemes taught, or provide some sentences on the interactive whiteboard that contain a missing word. Children have to work out the missing word and write it on their whiteboards with their partner's help.

● Make constant reference to robot talk, or the puppet who can only speak in phonemes, to support children in writing words, so that they realise they first need to split the word into phonemes orally and then write corresponding graphemes.

You Can... **Help children talk like a robot**

The synthetic phonics approach revolves around saying the phonemes in isolation and then blending them together to make words. Alongside the ability to blend the phonemes is the reversible process of segmenting a word into its constituent phonemes. This is a complex skill which can be helped by introducing the idea of talking in a staccato way like a robot.

Thinking points

● Once you have introduced the idea of robot talk, you will need to incorporate this into all phonics sessions, so that children have the opportunity to practise segmenting words alongside blending them for reading. The main aim of learning to segment words is to support children's ability to spell words. It should therefore be introduced early in a systematic phonics programme and then developed as children learn and apply all the 44 phonemes.

● Another way of approaching the concept of segmenting words is to talk about a secret code. Some children may have come across the idea of codes through television and film. You can then have fun talking in code – that is, in phonemes – with children replying to you in the same code.

Tips, ideas and activities

● Using a picture, introduce a robot who can only talk in phonemes. You may like to give the robot a name, such as 'Ruby Robot'. The following is an example of how this might be done using robot talk:

- This is Ruby and, because she is a robot, she talks in a strange way. Let's hear her talk.
- /s/a/d/ *(hold up the picture of robot and pretend it is talking)*
- What do you think she said? Can you repeat it?
- Yes /s/a/d/. What does she mean? Is she sad? Well done! Yes, she says 'sad'.
- Now she does not understand you unless you talk like a robot. You need to say the sounds – remember we call them 'phonemes' – separately. Shall we have a go? Let's try with pin. Good it's /p/i/n/. Can you say that to Ruby? Let's see if she says it back to you.
- /p/i/n/.
- Well done! Remember, when we talk to Ruby we must talk in phonemes.

● Use a puppet who can only speak in phonemes. Through the puppet, say words in individual phonemes, for example /s/u/n/, and ask the children to tell their partner the word. Encourage the children to talk to the puppet in phonemes, repeating it several times until the puppet gets it right!

● Ask the children to pretend to be robots and work in pairs. Give them time to think of words (or provide some) and then to say them like a robot to their partner. Their partner should guess what the word is.

You Can... **Ensure plenty of oral work**

Underpinning the learning of phonics is the ability to listen effectively and to be able to hear and enunciate phonemes correctly. Children therefore need to have plenty of opportunities for practice at saying the sounds and orally blending them. Speaking and listening activities are at the heart of any phonic programme. It is important to ensure that the emphasis is on oral work, only teaching letter formation and making links to writing the corresponding graphemes where appropriate.

Thinking points

● When conducting phonic sessions, do you ensure that children all get the chance to practise saying the phonemes? Asking children to sit in a circle and take turns in a specific activity, such as saying an initial sound in a word, can support this.

● Consider also whether you have efficient systems for monitoring children's ability to enunciate phonemes correctly as well as the developing skill of blending phonemes for reading. If you have additional adults in the classroom or early years setting, either identify specific children for them to observe or ask them to provide additional activities with small groups.

● Make use of incidental moments in the day to reinforce oral work with songs and rhymes or blending/segmenting phonemes, for example by talking to a puppet.

Tips, ideas and activities

● Play games such as 'I went to market and I bought…' with items that all start with the same initial phoneme (for example, sausages, soap, scissors, Sellotape).

● Look at games that require lively oral activities. Some examples are provided in *Progression in Phonics* (DfES, 1999), such as 'Mood sounds' where the children have to say a phoneme in a certain way (as if they are sad, angry, happy, and so on). Another example is 'Noisy letters' where children are given a letter card which they hold so no one can see. They then say the common sound that letter makes. Continuing to make that sound, they walk around until they group with others making the same sound.

● When helping children to identify the number of phonemes in a word, try different ways of doing this. For example, say a word, ask the children repeat it, then together tap out the number of phonemes on parts of the body, such as heads, shoulders or knees.

● Encourage links to role play by using different puppets, for example one puppet speaks in phonemes and another speaks in full words. You will need to work with another child to demonstrate this and then encourage children to explore themselves.

● Make links to a speaking and listening corner in the classroom or setting where tapes of songs and rhymes are available. Also provide alphabet books and puzzles so that children can work together and support their growing knowledge of the alphabet.

● Make links to outdoor active games, such as hopping over certain letters drawn on the ground and saying the phoneme (in a similar way to hopscotch).

You Can... **Use partner work**

The use of partner work is a powerful tool for learning in a range of ways. The Primary National Strategy guidance (2006, page 27) states that 'through peer marking and talking partners, children are encouraged to share their phonic knowledge to reinforce learning'. The advantages of partner work are that it encourages maximum participation in all activities and that children can support each other in their learning. It will also aid children's personal, social and emotional development through helping them to interact positively with others.

Thinking points

● Working with a partner will require the teaching of specific skills, for example, looking at your partner and taking turns to talk. Consider whether to develop specific partnerships or make this flexible so that children will turn to the person next to them.

● This can be linked to the use of the think/pair/share strategy. This is where you ask the children to think of an answer to your question, give them time to do this (this is important), and then ask them to share their ideas with their partner. Once they have had a few minutes to do this, ask them to show they are ready to share. This can be done by holding their partner's hand up (as opposed to a single hand up). Then choose a few partners to share their answers.

Tips, ideas and activities

● Paired reading can be part of normal activities. For example, children can use decodable books and practise taking turns at reading a sentence or a page at a time. Choose children carefully for these activities, considering whether you want to pair those of similar reading ability or sometimes ask a more proficient child to support one who needs additional practice.

● Paired writing using mini-whiteboards can also be very useful. Working with a small group or class, say a word which incorporates phonemes taught and ask the children to write it on whiteboards. Provide one pen and whiteboard per pair, asking the children to take turns to write the words. Children show you the words they have written, providing valuable opportunities to monitor their progress and use any errors as teaching points, for example, where an incorrect spelling choice has been made (such as the letter 'k' for 'kar' instead of 'c').

● Paired writing can be extended to working in a variety of ways. Try creating books (for example, alphabet books) or writing sentences with words that you provide in the wrong order – the children have to first help each other to put the words into a sensible order and then write the sentences.

● Partner work can also be supported by the use of magnetic letters and boards to build words, for example, 'to – top – stop'. You may like to provide a limited number of letters corresponding to phonemes taught and ask children to work together to see how many words they can make. Use examples of 'non-words' to highlight the children's skills in blending, although make sure you explain that these are not real words.

You Can... **Ensure children always hear, say, read and write phonemes**

The interconnection of reading, writing and speaking and listening for learning phonics is emphasised in the Rose Report (2006) which states: 'Speaking and listening, together with reading and writing, are prime communication skills that are central to children's intellectual, social and emotional development. All these skills are drawn upon and promoted by high quality, systematic phonic work' (DfES, 2006, page 3). Making clear the links between oral and written work, underpinned by phonic knowledge, helps children to build a store of words which in turn helps their comprehension skills.

Thinking points

● Include a rich diet of rhyming stories and poems, encouraging children to join in when possible. This will support children's understanding of rhyme, encourage them to repeat them and make links between oral and written work.

● As the *Rose Report* makes clear, reading ability centres on two main aspects: language comprehension and word recognition. It is vitally important to develop children's comprehension skills alongside discrete teaching of phonics. Rose states: 'As reading comprehension has now been shown to depend crucially on language comprehension, teachers also need to have good knowledge and understanding of oral language development, and of ways to foster language comprehension.' (2006, page 39) Language comprehension is developed through interaction and conversation and is supported by a wide range of texts and work across the curriculum.

Tips, ideas and activities

● Following the guidance for the structure of phonic sessions, as set out on page 18, will ensure that clear links are made between oral and written work. Children hear, say, read and write phonemes as they are taught, applying their newly learned skills.

● Model making the links by reading a decodable text together and then writing some further sentences together in shared writing. This provides valuable opportunities to model saying sentences aloud first before writing them, taking children's suggestions for spelling the words as you write. Guided writing sessions with children can further support their writing of their own sentences.

● The Reading Recovery method of supporting children's reading, which originated from the work of Marie Clay (1979), makes strong links between speaking and listening, reading and writing. The format of a typical Reading Recovery lesson provides useful guidance for making links from phonics sessions:
  ◦ Read familiar stories.
  ◦ Read a story that was read for the first time the day before.
  ◦ Work with letters and/or words using magnetic letters.
  ◦ Write a story.
  ◦ Assemble a cut-up story.
  ◦ Introduce and read a new book.
Use these principles to reinforce phonic knowledge, particularly linking reading decodable text and writing sentences that incorporate phonemes taught.

● Use of favourite stories can also be an excellent way of reinforcing phonics skills. Have fun with the sounds of words, and make links to specific phonemes taught.

You Can... **Help children practise reading decodable words**

The Rose Report clearly sets out the place of decodable books (DfES, 2006, page 27,), stating that children 'should be given reading material that is well within their reach in the form of "decodable books", that is to say, early reading books specially designed to incorporate regular text, which children can decode using the phonic skills they have secured.' The reason is that 'this enables them to benefit from "quick wins" in practising phonic skills and gaining confidence from reading a whole, albeit short, book.'

Thinking points
● One of the main advantages of using decodable books is that children are able to practise blending phonemes. Providing simple books that children can decode (either published or ones you create) means they can then be sent home for parents to help children as reinforcement.

● Ensure that alongside decodable books you are providing a rich literacy environment with access to a wide range of children's books.

● Examples of repeated text in some children's books such as *We're Going on a Bear Hunt* by Michael Rosen and Helen Oxenbury (Walker Books) can also support decoding of simple text.

● You may like to point out some words that can easily be decoded and then do this together. Such books can therefore be used in parallel.

Tips, ideas and activities
● The use of mini-books that contain simple decodable text at a level that is appropriate for young children is a valuable tool for practising blending phonemes. You may like to create your own books by folding several A4 pages in half and stapling along the left-hand edge. On each page, write simple sentences using phonemes you have taught. For example, for the phonemes /s/a/t/p/i/n/ you could create the words: tap, sat, pin, at, pat, nap, nip, ant, pant, in, an. The following simple sentences could be written into mini-books:

An ant sat.	Pat an ant.
Sat on a pin.	Tap, tap, tap.
In a pin.	In a tap.
Nip, nip, nip	...an ant.

● In your mini-books, include a few irregular words that are taught as 'sight words', such as 'the' or 'was'. This will extend the range of sentences you can create. Ensure you limit such words to a minimum as the emphasis should be on the children blending the majority of words. For parents' benefit, you may wish to print on the book cover: 'Words that children will need help with are: the, we, of.'

● You may like to encourage children to create their own illustrations for their mini-book after having read each sentence. Alternatively, you could incorporate a range of pictures obtained from clip art.

● The use of captions and messages within the context of role play can also support children's decoding of print. Indeed, a print-rich environment is a key part of every early years classroom or setting. Ensure you encourage children to engage with the print, modelling how to read example captions. Examples could be:

You can play in the sand.	Make a list
Hop on the mat.	Clap and sing.

You Can... **Encourage children to apply phonics when writing**

In order to support children's learning of phonics, it is important for them to apply their phonic knowledge, not only by reading words (by blending phonemes), but also by writing words. This involves the process of saying the word, orally segmenting it into phonemes, and then writing the corresponding graphemes. Children should therefore be encouraged to apply this skill whenever they are writing in a wide range of contexts. This should be supported by frequent modelling of writing in front of the children.

Thinking points

● Incorporate reading and writing words in all phonics lessons, using the format of 'Hear it, say it, read it, write it'. This provides constant reminders of applying phonic knowledge as well as reinforcement of different ways of remembering phonemes taught.

● Encourage children's early attempts at writing, developing from mark making to more recognisable letters. It is easy for young children to feel discouraged due to the complexity of not only the ability to match the correct graphemes to phonemes, but also the ability to form the letters and write them correctly.

● When children have been taught a few phonemes and their corresponding graphemes, support them in using them in a range of writing. For example, when they are attempting to write a word, say the phoneme and ask them what letter(s) they need, then encourage them to try and write the letter, perhaps pointing out examples of letters in the classroom.

Tips, ideas and activities

● One of the keys to supporting children in applying their phonic knowledge when writing is by modelling writing. Providing regular opportunities when you write in front of the children on an easel or whiteboard is crucial. This can be done in a range of contexts, for example you may have regular news-writing sessions, where children tell you something they have done at home. You then write a child's sentence on the easel encouraging the children to help you. One example could be:

- Jamal's sentence is: 'I went to the seaside.'
- Now which word do I start with? Yes, 'I'.
- How do I start every sentence? Yes, with a capital letter.
- Now I need to write 'went'. What letter does this start with?

And so on, constantly asking children to help you and apply their phonic knowledge.

● Once you have modelled examples of writing, it is very helpful for children to have a go themselves. Support this process by including partner work. Begin by asking children to say their sentence to their partner. When they are happy with their sentence, ask them repeat it into their own cupped hands. The children now hold the sentence tight in their hands and move to tables in order to write it in their books. The physical process of doing this does seem to help them recall what to write!

● Creating writing areas in the classroom is another way of encouraging children to write. Provide a range of paper, books and pens/pencils and allow them to experiment. You may also like to provide examples of mini-books for them to write in.

● Ensure that role-play activities in the classroom also incorporate opportunities for writing, such as message pads, lists and diaries.

You Can... # Use puppets

Using puppets with young children is a fun way of encouraging them to engage with learning phonics. Young children will often respond to a puppet where they might be reluctant to say something to a teacher or adult. It is often fascinating to see that, in spite of a lack of ventriloquist's skills by an adult, children do believe it is the puppet talking! Children can also be encouraged to use the puppets themselves, for example, to practise talking in phonemes.

Thinking points

● Collect a range of puppets to be used in a variety of ways. You may find that charity shops or car boot sales are a useful resource. You will also find a range of suppliers on the internet (for example at www.thepuppetman.co.uk).

● Do you have special puppets in the classroom? Do you use them to encourage all children to participate?

● Provide opportunities for children to play with the puppets, having fun in different ways. For example, use a puppet theatre and ask two children to play with one puppet each. Observe their interactions carefully and intervene at key 'teachable moments'. Make links to phonics teaching where appropriate.

Tips, ideas and activities

● One successful example of using puppets is to have a puppet who makes mistakes and cannot articulate sounds correctly. There is a good example of this, using a puppet called 'Croaker' and relating to teaching final phonemes in words, in the *Progression in Phonics* video and supporting materials (DfES, 1999). A similar principle can be used for a range of different aspects of phonics teaching. The puppet could say the wrong phoneme for the initial, medial or final sounds. Ensure that you emphasise the correct articulation and that the children say the sound correctly several times to the puppet. Be careful when teaching long vowel phonemes that any regional differences in pronunciation do not cause confusion.

● Another very useful way of using puppets is to have a puppet that can only speak in phonemes (in a similar way to robot talk, see page 36). Some phonics programmes recommend a particular puppet that is given a class name and even dressed in a school jumper! The children get very attached to the puppet and are keen to talk to him or her using phonemes. It can therefore be a useful incentive to have a class puppet for reinforcement of segmenting words into phonemes.

● Finger puppets can be used effectively with children in a variety of ways, for example:
  ○ Provide 'Phoneme finger puppets' where one grapheme corresponding to a taught phoneme is written on a finger puppet. Provide children with three finger puppets and ask them to make CVC words. This will require them to put the letters (puppets) in the correct sequence on their fingers and then, as they point to each, they say the corresponding phoneme and then blend into a word.
  ○ Have a range of finger puppets available for children to explore. Observe and intervene sensitively to encourage children to apply their growing phonic knowledge.

You Can... **Use actions**

The use of multi-sensory methods of learning has been shown to be particularly effective in teaching phonics. This has also been noted in the Rose Report (2006) and cited as good practice. Actions (alongside visual and auditory prompts) will reinforce children's learning and, as many children and adults respond differently according to preferred learning styles, it can be particularly helpful to incorporate a range of multi-sensory techniques. It is interesting to note how introducing an action alongside a particular phoneme helps children to remember that phoneme. Every time that phoneme is referred to thereafter, children soon recall the actions.

Thinking points

● Some published phonics programmes incorporate a range of actions. One of the key points is to be consistent in teaching the same action for each phoneme. In addition, you may wish to develop your own actions, particularly when learning the alphabet, so that together with the children you devise actions for each letter.

● Use incidental moments in the day to reinforce saying a phoneme and a corresponding action. This over-learning can be supportive for children as they work through a fast paced phonics programme.

Tips, ideas and activities

● To support learning the alphabet, in addition to learning a song, putting actions to different letters can act as reinforcement. For example:

R is for robot, rabbit, rat and Rick
(move stiffly like a robot)
S is for sun, sand and slithery snakes
(move arm like a snake)
T is for Thomas, tap, tent and takes
(tap your neighbour)
U is for uncle, us and umbrella
(put an umbrella up)

Provide regular practice, for example, by beginning every phonics session in the early stage with reciting an alphabet rhyme and doing the actions.

● As you work through a systematic phonics programme, introduce each new phoneme accompanied by actions:
1. Introduce a phoneme by showing a range of pictures or objects that represent that phoneme (/n/ – nets, nuts and nests). Children say what each begins with.
2. Say an alliterative phrase ('Nets catch nuts and nests').
3. Teach the corresponding action (pretend to throw a nut and catch in a net). Children then go on to enunciate the phoneme, read the grapheme and then write it, followed by simple words that contain the phoneme.

● When teaching long vowel phonemes, it is particularly helpful to use multi-sensory techniques as these phonemes are the most complex to learn. A rhyme or rap can be taught for each phoneme accompanied by an action, as follows:
1. Say the phoneme twice (/ay/ay/).
2. Say the mnemonic (Play with hay).
3. Say the letter names (A, Y).
4. They do the action (pretend to lift a pile of hay).

The rap then builds up as each phoneme is learned.

You Can... Use songs and rhymes

Using a range of rhymes and songs is common practice in early years teaching. Used alongside a systematic phonics programme they can be valuable reinforcement of specific phonemes. Not only are they fun, so children readily engage with them, but also the act of singing particularly aids recall. Classic texts, such as This Little Puffin compiled by Elizabeth Matterson, are on most practitioners' shelves, and we should not forget their potential in supporting the teaching of phonics.

Thinking points

● As mentioned on pages 9–12, the use of a range of rhymes is an important way of developing phonological awareness, that is being able to identify and distinguish individual sounds.

● Do you continue to use rhymes and songs throughout your phonics programme? They can be useful, not only for emphasising initial phonemes, but also for CVC words, consonant blends and long vowel sounds. In addition, rhymes can highlight that words may sound the same but can be spelt differently.

● Make use of incidental moments in the day to sing songs or say rhymes. They can be very useful in calming children down, by providing a quiet finish to a session. Alternatively, they can be accompanied by lively actions, such as marching up the hill in 'The Grand Old Duke of York'.

Tips, ideas and activities

● Use a wide range of nursery rhymes to support work on ensuring phonological awareness.

● Sharing rhyming stories is another way of encouraging the use of rhyme in connection with work on phonological awareness. Examples include: *Ten in the Bed* by Penny Dale (Walker Books), *The Dog that Dug* by Jonathan Long and Korky Paul (Red Fox), *The Trouble with Mum* by Babette Cole (Mammoth), *Pass the Jam, Jim* and *You Can Swim, Jim* by Kaye Umansky and Margaret Chamberlain (Red Fox), *Each Peach Pear Plum* by Janet and Allan Ahlberg (Puffin). In those texts which include repeated refrains, some words may be decoded phonetically.

● Selecting rhymes to support work on different phonemes can be very useful. Such rhymes can be particularly useful for supporting work on CVC words. For example:
> Higglety, piggelty, pop!
> The dog has eaten the mop.
> The pig's in a hurry,
> The cat's in a flurry,
> Higglety, piggelty, pop!

You could then work on other CVC words that rhyme with pop – mop, top, shop, cop, hop, lop, and so on.

● Using songs to support learning of either discrimination of sounds or teaching of specific phonemes can also be very helpful, for example:
> Oh I do like to be beside the seaside... tiddley om, pom, pom (final phoneme /m/)
> Ten in a bed... (final phoneme /d/)

● Poems that show how the same phoneme can be spelt in different ways can also be useful teaching tools. For example, the R L Stevenson poem 'Cows' shows alternative spellings of /ar/ as 'heart' or 'tart', /ie/ in 'white' and 'igh' in 'might, also /air/ as 'there' and 'air'.

You Can... **Use whiteboards**

Teaching phonics requires only a few resources. The most useful, as it can be adapted in a range of ways, is a set of mini-whiteboards (and pens), in addition to magnetic letters. Whiteboards will be needed in most phonics lessons so that children can practise writing the graphemes that correspond to the phoneme being taught. This will aid ongoing assessment of children's developing knowledge.

Thinking points

● When using whiteboards, do you include regular opportunities for children to work with a partner (one whiteboard and pen between two children)? This encourages children to support each other's learning. At other times, provide individual whiteboards, particularly when checking children's ability to spell words or form the letters correctly.

● You will need to ensure that whiteboards are wiped after use and that pens work. Ask children to help with this job, checking pens and giving out/collecting in whiteboards.

● Magnetic letters are particularly helpful as they are tactile and encourage children to feel the physical representation of the letters and to manipulate them into different combinations.

Tips, ideas and activities

● Providing whiteboards for pairs of children, or at times individuals, can be very useful as support when writing words containing the phoneme being taught. The process enables practice at forming the letters and segmenting words into their constituent phonemes and then writing the corresponding graphemes. Aim to incorporate this within every lesson by the following process:

1. Say a word containing the phoneme being taught and other learned phonemes (eg the word 'tap' for /t/). Children repeat the word.
2. Now ask children to split the word – segment it – into phonemes (eg /t/a/p/). They should say each phoneme, counting on their fingers the corresponding number.
3. They then show you how many phonemes (eg three for 'tap').
4. Now ask them to write the word on their whiteboards and then to show you.

● Use whiteboards to carefully note children's ability to segment words into phonemes and to write the correct letters. Note any children who require reinforcement and provide additional support.

● Magnetic letters and magnetic whiteboards can be a very useful resource for teaching phonics as you can provide the letters that correspond to the phonemes being taught. Say a word and ask the children to work in pairs to make the word using the letters that you have supplied. Repeat for several different words. This will support children's skills of segmenting by selected letters to make words. It will also support work on blending, as they can practise sliding letters together to make words.

● For each of the above, it is useful if the alphabet is displayed

You Can... **Use objects and pictures**

either on the whiteboards or clearly visible near to the children.

The use of a range of objects and pictures to support learning phonics is common practice. However, these need to be used as part of a systematic phonic programme and not part of a 'sound a week' teaching method. Previously, teachers would often have a table displaying objects and pictures related to the phoneme taught. This detracted from the need to teach phonics fast and early, as soon as children have demonstrated an ability to hear and discriminate individual sounds.

Thinking points

- Pictures and objects, carefully used within a systematic phonics programme, can support the learning of phonemes. The constant and rapid review of phonemes learned is a powerful tool to help children remember the phonemes. This is particularly the case with the complex long vowel phonemes.

- Pictures and objects enable the use of multi-sensory teaching. As you teach each phoneme, ensure that children have opportunities to associate it with a visual image, carry out an action and hear a phrase or rhyme that supports the learning.

- Pictures that relate to building a chart of phonemes can also present a strong visual image of the relation of different phonemes to each other. This is especially the case for the long vowel phonemes where there is a range of ways of spelling the phoneme.

Tips, ideas and activities

- Use pictures to accompany learning the alphabet in the form of a frieze, so children point to the pictures as they say/ sing the song.

- Objects are useful for playing games, for example the 'Tray game' from *Progression in Phonics* (DfES, 1999). In this game you have a selection of objects, some that relate to a specific initial phoneme and some that do not. Children decide which objects should go on the tray (that is, those that begin with the allotted phoneme).

- Use pictures and objects when introducing the consonants and short vowel phonemes, alongside saying the word. For example, for the phoneme /m/, you might have pictures of a man, monkey, mask, mat. Emphasis the initial sound when showing each picture, for example, 'mmmmman'.

- Cards for each phoneme taught can be very useful for constant reference. For consonant and short vowel phonemes these should contain an alliterative phrase for each phoneme and a picture that represents that phrase. The advantage of using these cards is that it supports over-learning, so that you can review phonemes taught each day by quickly holding up the cards, saying the alliterative phrase and the phoneme.

- When learning long vowel phonemes, the use of cards will again be a powerful tool for constant review. These should contain the phoneme, a short rhyme containing the phoneme, and the appropriate graphemes.

- Use these cards for constant review with the children. You may also like to use them to create a long vowel chart, putting underneath each other the different spelling choices for the same phoneme.

You Can... # Develop an effective assessment system

The Rose Report highlights the importance of developing an effective system which is 'simple, rigorous and purposeful' (paragraph 61). It is important to assess the children after each step has been taught to ensure the success of the teaching activities and that the time allowed for each step has been sufficient to achieve success. In this way, it is easy to diagnose any problems. You can than re-teach or consolidate, providing specific and alternate activities to address the difficulties. It is important that each stage has been achieved to ensure the children are confident and fluent and are therefore ready to move onto the next.

Thinking points

● Assessment falls into two categories: whole class and individual. Phonics can be assessed by stage and by individual categories.

● **Whole class.** Most schools assess their children towards the end of the year, in June, in order to pass on records to the new class teacher. For each class teacher, new targets will be set in September and revised each term.

● **Individual targets.** These are important to track the progress of each child and so measure the success of the teaching and the child's learning. Effective target setting is a mixture of testing, analysing and teacher expertise.

● Remember, problems with articulation, visual and auditory memory, and fine motor skills may have a physical cause which may need further investigation.

Tips, ideas and activities

● Try to use different examples for the assessment sheets. This will ensure that children do not make a learned response. Ensure that they are familiar with the format of the assessment sheets and always give an example to ensure complete understanding of expectations.

● Ensure that instructions are clear and standardised – that is, you give the same instruction to each child.

● Try to give pictures wherever possible to aid comprehension, especially in the early stages of testing phonics.

● A simple rule of thumb is to test blending skills with nonsense words, but test spelling with real words. The reason is that words can by recognised by sight and so you cannot be sure if the child is able to blend the sounds or is simply recalling the word by sight. However, recalling sounds for spelling is linked to visual memory, so real words have to be used.

● Photocopiable page 59 is an example of an overview record sheet. You should complete this periodically by dating when a child can read and spell consonant clusters or digraphs.

● Photocopiable 60 is an example pupil sheet. It should be used for pupils to read from in order to test blending (with nonsense words). This sheet is designed for use at an early stage in a phonics scheme as children learn the most common consonant and short vowel phonemes (/s/a/t/p/i/n/).

You Can... Assess good listening

The ability to listen is an essential prerequisite skill in the development of language and therefore of reading and writing, particularly phonological development. It is essential that those children who may have difficulties are identified early so a process of remediation can take place. There are many factors that can affect a child's ability to listen effectively: their previous experiences of listening may not match the school's expectations; there may be physical or neurological difficulties; the child may have a language difficulty and lack understanding as a result; or there may be motivational and emotional factors which will affect the child's ability to pay attention.

Thinking points

For children who are causing concern, the following should be carried out:

● Check the child's hearing by talking to parents or carers to ascertain if a recent health check has identified any difficulties. If not, suggest that one is done.

● Check their understanding of a range of simple vocabulary or give simple instructions and see if they can carry them out. If you are concerned, discuss with parents the advisability of referral to a speech therapist.

● Practise active listening, using visual cues to support the message – sitting still, looking at the speaker, thinking about the words (see page 7).

● Introduce activities that require a response (see below right for details). These include oral comprehension, auditory odd-one-out, word association games, following instructions, barrier/screen games, taped activities, simple Simon says, when you hear... (a particular name in a story, a number I say, etc) ... clap.

Tips, ideas and activities

● To make any assessment it is very important that although the format of the assessment is clearly understood and familiar to the child, the content of the assessment is fresh.

● Make sure that the environment is quiet and free from distraction.

● Give examples at the time of the assessment. For example:
  ○ 'We are going to play a listening game. I am going to play one of these instruments'. Show the child a tambourine, whistle and drum.
  ○ 'Show me your picture of the drum (for example).'
  ○ 'Listen to their sound. Show me the picture when you hear their sound.' Ensure they can identify sound to picture.
  ○ 'Now I'm going behind this screen. When you hear the sound, hold up the picture of the instrument that makes the sound.'

● Use hands and feet to coordinate a regular rhythm, for example, stamp your feet twice, clap once. Keep a record of the patterns so it can be repeated exactly for all the children.

● Use a tambourine to make heavy and soft beats using palms of hands and fingers. Play simple repetitive rhythms: /// /// /// /// /// (three beats repeated).

● Have a variety of objects in front of the child and a basket. Ask them to select items in the order you say and put them in a basket. Start from one item and build up to three or four items at once.

● Use pictures showing places such as the park, seaside, supermarket and school. Ask the children to draw a journey you describe by drawing a line on the picture.

You Can... **Assess good rhyming skills**

The ability to segment sounds and to identify, organise and recall similar sounds is paramount in the teaching of phonics. The first step is the ability to identify rhymes and then to gradually identify the parts of the words which rhyme. This is an ongoing process and for some children this awareness is only developed when they see the patterns in words. The teaching of rhyme and assessment of rhyme is therefore very important and should begin early in Foundation Stage and continue throughout the whole of Key Stage 1.

Thinking points

● When assessing, always start with examples that you carry out with children. This will give the children the opportunity to 'tune into' the exercise.

● Give the same examples to each child you test in order to ensure parity.

● Try to say the same words to make the assessment fair, for example 'I am going to say some words and I want you to tell me which two words sound the same at the end. Listen. Hat, pen, fat.' Repeat if necessary. If the child gives the wrong answer say, 'Hat and pen have a different sound at the end. Let's try another.'

● Use picture cards to help support auditory memory as you carry out rhyming tests.

Tips, ideas and activities

● Begin with oral activities. Can the children join in with nursery rhymes? Try a range and observe children carefully. See if they can say a range of nursery rhymes independently. (See page 9 for further activities.)

● The next step is to see if they can supply the missing word in a nursery rhyme, for example:
Pussy cat, pussy cat, where have you been?
I've been up to London to look at the...

● Try also seeing if children can identify a deliberate mistake in a nursery rhyme, for example, 'Jack and Jill went up the stairs'.

● Provide a range of pictures of objects that rhyme, for example, cat and hat. Can they identify a matching rhyme from three pictures, for example, hat, cat, leg?

● Play 'Snap'. Ask the child to listen and, if the words sound the same (rhyme), say 'snap'. Say the words, two at a time, for example, 'pin, tin' ... 'pat, cup'.

● Find out if they can continue a rhyming string, for example 'fan, man, can, Dan, ran'. Acceptable answers are words with the same sounds, not necessarily the same spelling patterns, for example, 'cake', 'break'.

You Can... Assess phoneme discrimination and initial phonemes

When children are able to identify words, they need to know that words are made up of phonemes. There are 26 graphemes (letters) in the alphabetic code and they represent 44 phonemes. Children also need to know that upper-case and lower-case letters represent the same phoneme, but letters such as 'b', 'd', 'p' represent different phonemes. Therefore children need to be able hear the sound in a word, recall the sound when they see the grapheme (letter) and represent the grapheme accurately when they hear the sound. There are also two choices, upper case or lower case, depending on the context of the word in the sentence.

Thinking points

● It is essential that the children are fluent in recalling the phonemes and writing the 26 graphemes.

● Phonemes taught need to be pure, without the 'uh' sound added. Insist on perfection, for example, 'p' as a whisper not as 'puh'.

● Be aware of children's natural language and speech development.

● Identify any children with articulation difficulties. Do they require further assessment by the speech and language therapist? Where appropriate, speak to the parents and the SENCO.

● Identify any children with gross and fine coordination difficulties as this has an impact on their ability to represent the letters accurately and to discriminate between similar letter shapes.

● Assess vowel sounds at the beginning of a word and use the short vowel sounds only.

● Assess 'x' as a final sound and ensure the children can hear the final sounds in words before you test it.

Tips, ideas and activities

● Ask the child to listen to the word you say and then tell you the sound they hear at the beginning of the word. Choose simple monosyllabic words and avoid prolonging the first sound.

● Repeat the process with made-up words, for example, 'bec', 'sal', 'fet', 'mig'.

● Ask the child to look at a picture and tell you the phoneme the word begins with.

● From a small group of letters, ask the child to show you which letter makes a particular phoneme.

● Show a grapheme upper and lower case and ask the child the sound it makes in a word.

● Ask the child to look at the first letter at the beginning of the line. Point to the letter. The ask them to find all the letters that are the same along the line. For example:
    s m s a s t n s s a m s t
They could point to them or track them with a drawn line.

● Ask the child to write the letter that makes a particular phoneme from memory. Say 'Write down the letter that says...'

● Give the child a worksheet with pictures on it in boxes. Ask him or her to write under the pictures if they can hear that particular phoneme in the word.

You Can... **Assess syllable awareness**

Children need to be able to discriminate individual words from continuous speech. It is an important part of developing the fine discrimination skills that support phonological awareness. Once the children are able to identify words, they can begin to identify the syllables (beats) in them. This is an important skill for reading and spelling words. As with all assessment, it is important that the area where you are testing is quiet and free from distraction. If you are assessing the children at your desk ensure that the rest of the class are doing a quiet activity and do not need your attention.

Thinking points

● This section is closely linked with the assessment of good listening skills. Consider whether the children passed the assessments in the 'listening' section on page 48. Also important is their understanding of rhythm. Can they repeat a simple clapping beat?

● You can test the children informally, noting in particular those who appear to have difficulty during the lesson. Give those children plenty of further practice.

● Remember, not all children develop at the same rate, and this is especially true for phonological awareness.

● When you are asking the children to identify the syllables in the words, don't say the word slowly because it distorts the rhythm or stress of the word. This is especially true for a one-beat word and the children will confuse the phonemes in the word with its syllable.

Tips, activities, ideas
Word identification

● Ask the child to put a counter over each word that you write on a piece of 'sentence strip' card. (They do not have to read the words.) Say the words as you write them. Read the sentence again and ask the child to place one counter on each word as you read the sentence.

● Read another sentence to the child. Then ask them to point to each word as you read it again.

● Ask the child to tap the table when they hear a chosen word in a short passage, for example 'red' in 'little red hen'.

Syllable identification

● Oral assessment: play 'My turn, your turn'. Say a word at the normal pace, for example, 'acrobat'. Ask the child to repeat it. This will ensure s/he has heard the word correctly. The child then repeats the word again and claps the syllables as they say it.

● Ask the child to sort a variety of pictures into 'beat' categories. Ensure they know the names of all the pictures. Have three boxes or trays with the numbers on them. Use symbols, such as counters or stickers, to show the number value.

● Assess syllable identification orally by supplying a word, for example, 'dinosaur'. The child identifies the number of syllables (3) and then you ask, 'What does the first beat say?', 'What does the second beat say?', 'What does the last beat say?'

You Can... **Assess letter name knowledge and alphabetical order**

There are three skills to assess here: the knowledge of the letter names, matching the upper- and lower-case letters, and the sequential order of the alphabet. Usually, the first stage in teaching the alphabet takes the form of a rhyme. Gradually, the emphasis changes to ordering the alphabet letters, recalling their names without the use of picture clues and then matching upper and lower case. Sequencing helps to support both visual and auditory memory skills, and using wooden or plastic letters also helps kinaesthetic memory because the children can feel the shape of the letters. This is essential for dyslexic children and good practice for all children.

Thinking points

● Use picture cards to support the teaching. It is good whole-school practice if the school adopts one system to promote continuity for the children.

● Display the alphabet (upper and lower case and picture cues) in the classroom.

● Teach and assess in small steps and do not expect the children to learn the whole alphabet in one go.

● Teach the children to put out the alphabet arc, with 'A' at the beginning, 'M' in the middle and 'Z' at the end, using wooden or plastic letters.

● Use upper case for children who have letter reversal difficulties.

Tips, ideas and activities

● Using the alphabet frieze, can the children recite the alphabet rhyme up to the point you have taught it so far? A suggested order might be 'A–G', then 'A–M', 'A–S', 'A–Z'. This will depend on the rhyme and how it flows. Sit the children with their back to the frieze when testing or cover it with paper.

● Assess the children's ability to recall the letter names only, with you supporting them with an alphabet rhyme. So, in the following example, the children say the letter names and you say the rhyme :

A is for ants as well as for juicy apples
B is for balloon that shines and dapples
C is for cat, camel, cup and cake
D is for door, dog and drake

Assess the children's ability to point to each letter in the alphabet in order and recall its name, using wooden or plastic letters jumbled up.

● Find out if they can point to each letter in the alphabet and recall its name out of sequence.

● Can they point to each letter at random and recall its name?

● Put the letters you are assessing in a feely bag. Ask the children to put their hand in the bag and find you a particular letter.

● Can the children match the upper- and the lower-case letters?

● Using alphabet letters, can they sequence the letters 'A–G', 'H–M', 'N–S', 'T–Z'?

● Can the children track the letters in alphabetical order on a sheet of mixed letters?

You Can... **Assess consonant clusters and common consonant digraphs**

The step from identifying and reading three-letter blends to reading four-letter or five-letter blends is not always automatic. Children need to identify initial and final consonant blends as separate sounds for spelling, but they also need to be fluent in blending them for reading. They also need to recognise that some consonant patterns represent one sound – common digraphs. This requires a visual memory recall.

Thinking points

● Teach the blends as you introduce the letters both as an initial and final sound. For example:
    i, t, p, n, s, a = spin, tint, stint, past, tips

● Common digraphs to be assessed for reading and spelling include:

    'sh' as an initial and final sound
    'ch' as an initial and final sound
    'nch' and 'tch'
    'qu' spelling rule: after a 'q' is always a 'u'
    'th' voiced as in 'this', 'then', 'the' and unvoiced as in 'thin', both as an initial and final sound

Note: the 't' in 'tch' is hard to hear, so the children will need to learn the spellings of 'rich', 'such' and 'much' as the exceptions to the rule.

Tips, ideas and activities

● Initial consonant blends to be assessed for reading and spelling are: bl, br, cl, cr, dl, dr, fl, fr, gl, gr, pl, pr, spr, spl, str, squ, shr, st, sp, sc, sk, sl, sm, sn, sw.

● For each of these initial consonant clusters ascertain:
    1. Can the children hear the phonemes within the initial consonant clusters? (Use cards – read a word, the child says the blends, and points to a card with the blends on.)
    2. Can the children say the initial consonant clusters? (Use pictures – the child points to a picture, for example, a clown and says 'clown, cl').
    3. Can the child blend and read words (use nonsense words, see photocopiable page 60) with initial consonant clusters?
    4. Can the child write words with initial consonant clusters? (Use real words with short vowel sounds and known phonic sounds only.)

● Points 1–4 can be repeated to assess the final consonant blends and the common digraphs and can form targets.

● Final consonant blends to be assessed for reading and spelling are: st, sp, sn, nd, nt, nk, sk, ct, pt, ft, lt, lf, lk, lp, mp, xt, nch, tch.

● Common digraphs to be assessed for reading and spelling, both as initial and final sounds, are: sh, ch, th, qu.

● Keep a careful note of children's progress on an individual tracking form (see photocopiable page 61).

You Can... **Assess long vowel phonemes**

The long vowel phonemes in words can present children with the most difficulty. Long vowel sounds can be presented as open syllables ('he', 'she', 'me', 'I'), two vowels together ('ai', 'ay', 'ou', 'ie'), or as two vowels split by a consonant ('a_e', 'i_e', 'o_e', 'u_e'). Vowels can also be modified by a consonant to change its sound ('wa' 'ar', 'ir' 'or' 'ur', 'are', 'ire'). Constant practice and over-learning will support children's learning of these phonemes, as well as accurate individual assessment.

Thinking points

● Recalling vowel digraphs and modified vowel sounds require the child to use a visual memory strategy, so use a visual means to recall the sounds and write the words. For example, you cannot hear the difference between 'ai' and 'ay' in a word. The difference is in its use, therefore the children need to see the word in context. Use a mnemonic to help, for example, 'ee, ee, Feel the tree, EE'.

● Ensure the children can understand, recall and apply one set of long vowel phonemes before proceeding with the next step.

● Constantly assess and refer to any strategies you have implemented.

● Link spelling rules and syllable patterns with the teaching, for example: 'y' at the end of a one-beat word says 'I' (long sound)

● Linking high frequency words to the phonic lessons can also support children in learning these phonemes.

Tips, ideas and activities

● When testing, use cards for each of the long vowel phonemes that show the grapheme, a mnemonic and a corresponding picture. Ensure children recall the mnemonic and phoneme using the cards. Children should be able to turn them over quickly recalling both.

● Test whether the children identify and blend the long vowel phonemes in words (nonsense words ensure that they can identify the vowel digraph and can blend it in a word).

● Use the high frequency word list to identify words with long vowel phonemes that they have read.

● Check if the children identify and read words with long vowel sounds with modified sounds. (These need to be the real words.)

● Ensure that children write the phoneme from dictation. Say, 'Write me the letters that say /a/, as in "play with hay".'

● Use high frequency words where possible and read the word in a sentence to put it in its true context.

● The assessment sheet on photocopiable page 62 demonstrates one way of recording progress with this, and links with *Phonics: A Complete Synthetic Programme (Stage 3)* by Wendy Jolliffe (Scholastic Ltd).

You Can... **Develop an effective tracking system**

As highlighted by the Rose Report, one key aspect to phonics teaching is to accurately assess and to track children's progress in learning phonics. Your tracking system should be developed so that this information is transferred from Foundation Stage and throughout Key Stage 1. The system should be clear and simple to use and, when a child has provided evidence of clearly being able to identify specific phonemes and to blend them for reading and segment them for spelling, this should be recorded.

Thinking points

● Decide on a school-wide policy for recording children's progress linked to the scheme you are following. For example, in the *Primary National Strategy* guidance it is recommended children work through six phases:

Phase 1: phonological awareness

Phase 2: a small selection of common consonants and vowels

Phase 3: know one grapheme for each of the 44 phonemes

Phase 4: blend adjacent consonants in words and apply when reading by blending and segment for spelling

Phase 5: alternative spellings for long vowel phonemes

Phase 6: apply phonic skills with complex words and less common correspondences and irregularities

● Decide on how frequently children's progress will be recorded and what is recorded.

● Utilise this information for summative purposes, for example, the Foundation Stage Profile.

● Ensure that this information will, later in Key Stage 1 and Key Stage 2, feed into work on spelling.

Tips, ideas and activities

● Guidance on page 53 (and photocopiable pages 59–60) explained methods of phonic assessment for consonant clusters and consonant digraphs, and should be used alongside teaching a systematic phonics programme. Use these to provide an overview sheet (see page 47, on developing an effective assessment system). It is important to record that children are able to read and spell words containing the phonemes.

● The Primary National Strategy provides one example of a tracking sheet, broken into half-termly blocks to record progress. Another example of a tracking sheet is provided on photocopiable page 63. The key point is that schools will need to personalise their system to meet the programme taught.

● The key aspect is to use this data to inform future teaching, providing reinforcement for pupils where necessary.

Daily phonics lesson plan

1. Rhyme, song or rap (approximately 2–3 mins)
- Teach a rhyme, song or rap linked to the alphabet and practise with actions.

2. Review phonemes taught (approximately 5 mins)
a) Hear it
- Say words containing the phonemes taught in the initial position.
- Children say which phoneme they can hear.

b) Say it
- Say several words containing the phonemes taught, slowly in robot talk.
- Ask children to blend the phonemes into words.

c) Read it
- Point to a range of graphemes displayed on cards and ask children to tell you the phonemes.

d) Write it
- Ask children to write the graphemes as you say the phonemes.
- Practise writing words using phonemes taught.

3. New phoneme (8–10 mins)
a) Hear it
- Say a range of words containing the phoneme.
- Children say which phoneme they can hear.
- Reinforce with an alliterative phrase.
- Practise with an appropriate action.

b) Say it
- Reinforce correct pronunciation of the sound and practise saying it several times.
- Now you say several words containing the phoneme taught, using robot talk.
- Ask the children to blend the phonemes into words.

c) Read it
- Show the new letter card and say the phoneme. Add it to the display of others taught.

d) Write it
- Say the phoneme again and ask the children to write the letter.
- Provide cues for letter formation.
- Tell the children a word containing the new phoneme and others taught and ask them to write the word and show you.

Phoneme pronunciation chart

/s/	The mouth is slightly open and the tongue is flat behind your teeth. Air comes out between your teeth. You can stretch the sound.
/a/	Open your mouth wide and make a loud sound, as if something is nipping you /a/a/a/. You can stretch the sound.
/t/	Your mouth is open and your tongue is behind your teeth. It starts at the top of your mouth and goes down. Feel the air come out of your mouth as you do it. Make it a very short sound and whisper it.
/p/	Touch your lips together quickly. Imagine you are blowing a candle out on a cake and make it a very short sound and whisper it.
/i/	Open your mouth a tiny bit and the corners of your mouth pull back. You can stretch the sound.
/n/	The tip of your tongue goes behind your top teeth and your tongue doesn't move. You can stretch the sound.
/e/	Your mouth is open a little and your teeth are apart. It looks like you are smiling.
/d/	Put the tip of your tongue behind your top teeth and move your tongue down. It's a bit like /t/ but only a little air comes out of your mouth.
/m/	Put your lips together. It sounds like humming. You can stretch the sound.
/g/	Feel the sound right at the back of your mouth. Put your fingers on your throat and feel the sound.
/o/	Your mouth is open and your chin drops down a little. You can stretch the sound.
/k/	Feel the sound in the back of your mouth. It sounds a bit like /g/, but you can feel air coming out from your mouth and whisper it.
/u/	Open your mouth just a little. You need to push some air out as you do it.
/r/	Lift your tongue up in the back of your mouth. It sounds like a car going fast. You can stretch the sound.
/b/	When you make this sound your lips go together and pop open. It is like /p/ but no air comes out.
/f/	Touch your teeth onto your bottom lip and push air between your teeth. You can stretch the sound and whisper it.
/l/	Move your tongue to the top of your mouth. It stays there as you make the sound in the back of your mouth. You can stretch the sound.
/h/	Open your mouth a little. You push air out of your mouth to whisper it. You can stretch the sound.
/sh/	Put your teeth together and push air out of your mouth. You can stretch the sound.
/z/	Put your teeth together and your tongue near the front of your mouth and behind your teeth. You push air through your teeth and it makes a buzzing noise. You can stretch the sound.
/w/	Put your lips close together in a little circle, then open them up.
/ch/	Stick out your lips a little. Your teeth are together at first and then they open up.
/j/	Stick out your lips a little. Your tongue is near the top of your mouth and it moves when you open your mouth.
/v/	Touch your teeth onto your bottom lip and push air between your teeth. You can stretch the sound.
/y/	Open your mouth a little and put your tongue near the top of your mouth. Your tongue touches the sides of your teeth. Your mouth is open a little more at the end of the sound.
/th/	When you make the sound /th/ as in 'thin', put your tongue between your teeth and stick it out. Push air between your tongue and teeth. You can stretch the sound and whisper it.
/th/	When you make the sound /th/ sound as in 'this', your tongue touches the top of your mouth and it vibrates. Your can feel the sound in your throat. You can stretch the sound.
/ng/	This is like a humming sound at the back of your throat but you make it with your mouth open. You can stretch the sound.
/zh/	Open your lips in a little circle and blow air through your mouth. Your mouth opens wider at the end of the sound.

A phoneme chart

Consonant and short vowel phonemes	Common spellings	Long vowel phonemes	Common spellings
/s/	sun, mouse, city, mess, science, mice	/ae/	play, take, snail, baby
/a/	apple	/ee/	feel, heat, me
/t/	tap, better	/ie/	tie, fight, my, bike, tiger
/p/	paper, hippo	/oe/	float, slow, stone, nose
/i/	ink, bucket	/u/	took, could, put
/n/	noise, knife, gnat	/ue/	room, clue, grew, tune
/e/	egg, bread	/ow/	cow, loud
/d/	dog, puddle	/oi/	coin, boy
/m/	man, hammer, comb	/ur/	fur, girl, term, heard, work
/g/	game, egg	/au/	sauce, horn, door, warn, claw, ball
/o/	octopus, want	/ar/	car, fast (regional)
/c/, /k/	cat, Chris, king, luck, queen	/air/	hair, bear, share
/u/	umbrella, love	/ear/	ear, here, deer
/r/	rabbit, wrong, berry	/ure/	sure, tour
/b/	baby, cabbage	/er/	teacher, collar, doctor, about
/f/	fish, photo, coffee		**notes**
/l/	leg, spell		
/h/	hat		
/sh/	ship, mission, chef		
/z/	zebra, please, is, fizzy, sneeze		
/w/	water, wheel, queen		
/ch/	chip, watch		
/j/	jug, judge, giant, barge		
/v/	van, drive		
/y/	yes		
/th/	thin		
/th/	then		
/ng/	ring, sink		
/zh/	treasure		

Record of initial and final clusters to read and spell

Name _____   Class _____

Final consonant	Read	Spell
ck		
ll		
ss		
sh		
ch		
th		
ng		
ld		
nd		
lk		
nk		
sk		
lp		
mp		
sp		
ct		
ft		
lt		
nt		
pt		
st		
xt		
lf		
nch		
lth		

Initial consonant clusters	Read	Spell
bl		
br		
cl		
cr		
dr		
dw		
fl		
fr		
gl		
gr		
pl		
pr		
sc		
scr		
sk		
sl		
sm		
sn		
sp		
spl		
spr		
squ		
st		
str		
sw		
tr		
tw		
thr		
shr		

Vowel phonemes	Read	Spell
ee		
ea (eat)		
ai		
a_e		
ay		
ie (lie)		
i_e		
igh		
y (fly)		
oa		
oo (moon)		
o_e		
ow (grow)		
u_e		
ew		
ue (blue)		
oo (good)		
ar		
oi		
oy		

Vowel phonemes	Read	Spell
ow (brow)		
air		
are (care)		
ere (there)		
ear (pear)		
ear (fear)		
ea (head)		
or		
oor (moor)		
aw		
au		
ore		
all		
er		
ir		
ur		
ph		
wh		
ch (school)		

Assess the first
10 sounds and blends

Ask children to read these letters and nonsense words to test blending skills.

Example: Phonic 1 Week 2

s	a	t	p	i
n	e	d	m	g
sm	nd	nt	sp	st
sn	ss	tam	min	gep
mant	das	stap	spid	snep
pind	tiss	smid		

Phonics assessment 1

This is a teacher's recording sheet. Print the words on a separate sheet for the children to read.

Name: _____   Class: _____   Year: _____

2-week assessment

Date: _____   Sounds score: _____   Words score: _____

1. s	2. a	3. t	4. p	5. i
6. n	7. e	8. d	9. m	10. g
sm	nd	nt	sp	st
sn	ss	tam	min	gep
mant	das	stap	spid	snep
pind	tiss	smid		

6-week assessment

Date: _____   Sounds score: _____   Words score: _____

11. o	12. k	13. c	14. u	15. r
16. b	17. f	18. l	19. h	20. sh
sc	sk	ll	bl	fl
sl	pl	gl	cl	br
dr	pr	tr	cr	gr
fr	scr	spl	lp	mp
ft	bup	fen	lig	nell
ack	scam	skiff	blat	flig
slop	plut	clem	hud	shog
rab	brem	drot	treg	crub
holp	graf	frin	scrot	strim
splog	cush	leck	gisk	

12-week assessment

Date: _____   Sounds score: _____   Words score: _____

21. z	22. w	23. ch	24. j	25. v
26. y	27. th	28. qu	29. ng	30. x
wh	jit	vot	chig	rech
whit	yug	wib	thip	dath
bax	yav	moz	zen	quin

Phonics assessment 2

This is a teacher's recording sheet. Print the words on a separate sheet for the children to read. The words in brackets show the required sound for the digraph and for the nonsense word. If a child responds with another sound also made by the digraph, explain that this is correct, but ask if can they remember the other sound made by the digraph. Make a note of the response.

Name: _____   Class: _____   Year: _____

2-week assessment

Date: _____   Sounds score: _____   Words score: _____

Plus, test long vowel sounds: a, e, semi vowel y as in 'bony'/'fly' (test with real words).

ay	ai	ie	ee	ea (meat)
leem	gait	hieb	leat	spay
weaf	fay	reeb	laiv	diep

4-week assessment

Date: _____   Sounds score: _____   Words score: _____

Plus, test long vowel sounds: i, o, semi vowel y as in 'fly' (test with real words).

ie	igh	oa	ow
bie	zow	dight	poat
gow	noad	kie	digh

6-week assessment

Date: _____   Sounds score: _____   Words score: _____

Plus, test long vowel sound: u.

oo (moon)	ou	oo (book)	ue	ew
loon	lue	mew	mout	foom
prue	frew	doud	moy	wook

8-week assessment

Date: _____   Sounds score: _____   Words score: _____

a_e	i_e	o_e	u_e	ow (cow)	ou	oi	oy
boin	loid	jow	hode	nute	cate	libe	soy
sloud	tuve	doke	toit	froy	nide	jate	dow

10-week assessment

Date: _____   Sounds score: _____   Words score: _____

ur	ir	er	ear (hear/bear)	or	au	oor (moor)	ar
terv	boor	forb	burl	raud	carm	sirf	murl
mauv	harl	tirp	sie	vear	soor	derm	hork

12-week assessment

Date: _____   Sounds score: _____   Words score: _____

aw	ar	air	ear (hear/bear)	are	ere (there)	eer (deer)	ure	our
our	slaw	stear	sook	cleer	roat	ture	freer	gair
moad	mair	sare	plaw	rue	wook	nure	blear	tare

Phonics tracking record

Use this tracking sheet to note children's progress through the stages of phonics teaching, noting 'achieved' (A), 'partly achieved' (PA) and 'further reinforcement needed' (FRN) with dates.

Name: _____ **Class:** _____ **Year:** _____

Phonics stage	Term 1 Half term 1	Term 1 Half term 2	Term 2 Half term 1	Term 2 Half term 2	Term 3 Half term 1	Term 3 Half term 2
1. Phonological awareness: sounds, words rhyme, alliteration alphabet awareness						
2. Common consonants and short vowels (/s/a/t/p/i/n/)						
3. All consonant phonemes						
4. Long vowel phonemes						
5. Alternative spellings for long vowel phonemes						
6. Complex words, less common graphemes, phonic irregularities						

SCHOLASTIC

Also available in this series:

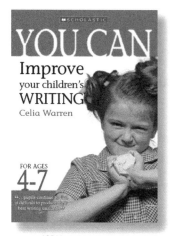

ISBN 0-439-94530-5
ISBN 978-0439-94530-1

ISBN 0-439-94531-3
ISBN 978-0439-94531-8

ISBN 0-439-94559-3
ISBN 978-0439-94559-2

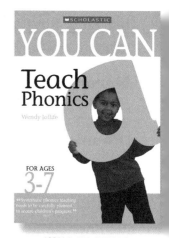

ISBN 0-439-94554-2
ISBN 978-0439-94554-7

ISBN 0-439-96522-5
ISBN 978-0439-96522-4

ISBN 0-439-96523-3
ISBN 978-0439-96523-1

ISBN 0-439-96534-9
ISBN 978-0439-96534-7

ISBN 0-439-96539-X
ISBN 978-0439-96539-2

ISBN 0-439-96540-3
ISBN 978-0439-96540-8

ISBN 0439-96554-3
ISBN 978-0439-96554-5

ISBN 0439-96555-1
ISBN 978-0439-96555-2

To find out more, call: 0845 603 9091
or visit our website www.scholastic.co.uk